Promoting Comprehensive Education in the 21st Century

Promoting Comprehensive Education in the 21st Century

Edited by Clyde Chitty and Brian Simon

Trentham Books

Stoke on Trent, UK and Sterling, USA

Trentham Books Limited

Westview House	22883 Quicksilver Drive
734 London Road	Sterling
Oakhill	VA 20166-2012
Stoke on Trent	USA
Staffordshire	
England ST4 5NP	

First published 2001

British Library Cataloguing-in-Publication Data
A catalogue record for this book is available from the British Library

ISBN 1 85856 253 8

Cover illustration: By kind permission of Steve Bell
© Steve Bell

Designed and typeset by Trentham Print Design Ltd., Chester and printed in Great Britain by Cromwell Press Ltd., Wiltshire.

Contents

Acknowledgements

The Editors would particularly like to thank the members of the Steering Group of the Conference from which this book springs:

Martin Allen, Jon Duveen, Richard Hatcher, Janet Holland, Alex Kenny, Mike Newman, Bernard Regan, Margaret Tulloch and Liz Williams.

They would also like to acknowledge the contribution of the following organisations who kindly sponsored the Conference: the Socialist Education Association (SEA), the Campaign for the Advancement of State Education (CASE), The Hillcole Group, *Forum* Journal, *Education and Social Justice* Journal and the Alliance for Inclusive Education.

Thanks also go to Margaret Brittain and Lesley Yorke for their help in the preparation of the manuscript in its final form.

1
Introduction

Clive Chitty and Brian Simon

Most of the chapters that appear in this book are the revised and edited versions of talks that were given at a conference with the title 'Promoting Comprehensive Education in the 21st Century', held at the University of London on the 3rd February 2001. This event was an outstanding success, attracting over 200 participants and setting the agenda for an alternative education policy based on the principles of equality, inclusion and social justice. Most of the talks by the main platform speakers are represented here; but it has not been possible to reproduce the lively and informed debates that took place during the afternoon workshop sessions which covered a wide variety of important subjects, including: selection, privatisation, curriculum and assessment, race and gender issues, special needs, accountability, community schooling, early years education and post-16 developments.

The book is divided into four main sections. Part One covers issues of selection and specialisation and the dangers inherent in the Government's obsession with its own narrow version of choice and diversity; Part Two concentrates on the growth of privatising tendencies with the attendant loss of democratic accountability; Part Three sums up the main themes and concerns of the Conference; and Part Four contains three important essays with particular relevance to the subject-matter of the volume.

The first chapter in Part One, by Geoff Whitty, attempts to identify some positive features in the present policy climate and argues for an acceptance that there is not just *one* model of comprehensive schooling and that contemporary society probably demands a greater degree of diversity and choice than may have been thought desirable in the past. Nevertheless, Professor Whitty accepts that New Labour's plans for specialisation within a broadly comprehensive system do not yet provide enough systemic safeguards to stop that agenda turning into a selective system in all but name. He argues for the rebuilding of a public education service based on collaboration between schools, communities and the relevant external agencies.

Clyde Chitty's analysis is rather more gloomy, suggesting that there is now *more* actual selection in the education system than existed in the immediate post-war period. He argues that the comprehensive reform has no meaning unless it challenges the fallacy of *fixed potential* in education – and that successive governments since the 1960s, both Labour and Conservative, have failed to dismantle the structures rooted in that fallacy. New Labour has inherited and built upon the Conservative policy of 'selection by specialisation'; and under the guise of *modernising* the comprehensive principle, is effectively *destroying* it.

Margaret Tulloch's piece concentrates on the failure of New Labour to end selection at 11-plus. The outcome of the Ripon ballot in March 2000 showed that campaigners against selection can expect no help from a Labour government. Carole Regan outlines some of the features of government policy that should form no part of 'a comprehensive agenda'; and Geoff Carr argues that the community school is the 'epitome' of comprehensive education because it provides the means for comprehensive schooling to tackle the agenda of social inclusion. The social inclusion/exclusion debate is also the concern of Rachel Jones who argues that the *Excellence in Cities* initiative will lead to a more diversified system of secondary schools. Mike Davies of the Human Scale Education Movement uses his experience as a co-director of Stantonbury Campus, Milton Keynes, in the 1980s to argue for the restructuring of large schools as part of a stronger and more popular future for comprehensive education. In a piece highlighting some of the divisive features of post-16 education, Jon Duveen and Philippe Harari argue that *comprehensive* post-16 education should allow all students to learn within the same coherent system, following a range of courses commanding equal levels of respect.

Part Two begins with a detailed and alarming account by Richard Hatcher of the privatisation of schooling. The existence of schooling as a publicly-run service is under threat from privatisation on a number of fronts, but this chapter concentrates on privatisation in the sense of private companies providing state education services for profit. The author argues that there are two logics clearly at work here: one is a logic of *business*, whose bottom line is obviously profit; the other is a logic of *education*, based on social and individual need and on concepts of equity and democracy. The crucial question for everyone concerned about the future of comprehensive schooling is: which logic shall predominate?

Richard Hatcher's case is supported by Bob Wood's piece telling the story of the campaign led by the Leeds Campaign for the Advancement of State Education (CASE) to keep a democratic and accountable education service in that city. And that is followed by a chapter by John Yandell, a secondary school teacher in East London, looking at some of the consequences of introducing a market system in education which sets student against student, teacher against teacher and school against school.

Part Three consists of a single paper, by Ken Jones, responding to some of the urgent themes of the Conference. This makes it clear that New Labour's education programme is not a local aberration and cannot be viewed in isolation from what is happening in a number of advanced capitalist countries. What we have to deal with is a major restructuring of education that more than ever subjects national policy to the vicious imperatives of market-driven globalisation. And 'joined-up government' needs to be confronted by 'joined-up opposition'.

Finally, Part Four consists of two additional essays which add weight to the general arguments of the volume. Brian Simon attacks the anti-comprehensive rhetoric in a recent speech on education by the Prime Minister, in an article which first appeared in the educational journal *Forum*; Tony Edwards and Patrick Eavis provide an in-depth study of the likely effects of a policy promoting curriculum diversity between schools.

Just over a week after the staging of the Conference (on the 12th February 2001), the Government published a major Green Paper on education: *Schools: Building on Success: Raising Standards, Promoting Diversity, Achieving Results*. This was intended to sum up the Government's educational 'achievements' since 1997 and, at the same time, set out the main objectives for a second term in office.

It is fair to say that this Green Paper served to justify many of the worst fears of the conference participants. It was discussed at a meeting of the main sponsors of the Conference which rejected its key proposals on the grounds that they *reinforced* an agenda that:

- continues to subject schools and colleges to a 'business knows best' culture, where 'failing' schools face privatisation and LEAs have been turned into business agents concerned with the outsourcing of services and where the private sector increasingly influences the direction of the education service as a whole.

- claims to promote 'school improvement', but fails to challenge the wider inequalities that have been the consequence of an education system driven by market forces, league tables and differential (and generally inadequate) funding.

- not only fails to challenge traditional forms of selection, but also extends it by increasing the number of 'specialist schools' able to recruit their own students and qualify for extra resources, while other schools struggle.

- terminates any commitment to a broad and balanced curriculum for all students in favour of one increasingly centred on 'basics', and where, in future, the academic-vocational divisions that continue to dominate post-16 education will become increasingly significant from the age of 14.

- despite all claims to the contrary, has seen New Labour spending less on education in every year of this parliament than its Tory predecessor spent in its last twelve months in power.

The vast majority of those speaking at and attending the February Conference would be able to unite around a manifesto which sought to actively defend the comprehensive principle and oppose privatisation, selection and the spread of specialist schools. Participants were able to articulate a vision of education for the 21st century where teaching and learning were based on the principles of equity and social justice rather than on ill-conceived notions of economic efficiency.

2

Foreword

Brian Simon

L ack of clarity, ambiguity and uncertainty among the Labour
Leadership and espousal of Tory policies, particularly as
defined in the 1988 Act are leading directly to the disastrous
polarisation of schools brilliantly exposed by Nick Davies in his
Guardian series on education.

Pailliatives, hurriedly concocted to cope with the resulting situation,
totally fail to measure up to the needs of the time. What is needed
now is clear thinking and decisive action, particularly on the key
issues of funding and admissions. On these and other, related, issues
there needs to be a return to first principles.

To get the crucial discussion started is the job of this book. There is
no more important issue in the whole field of education. The Prime
Minister tells us that secondary education is one of the three main
policy issues for Labour. Of course we all want 'modernisation' but
the term covers a multitude of sins. So does this mean we want a
two-tier system, now being constructed? Increased selection (by
'aptitude'), fast tracking, 'rigorous setting' (which sound like a
medieval form of torture), and the rest?

Certainly not. We want genuinely comprehensive schools serving
local communities in every area throughout the country. A unified
national system but under local, and democratic control. Not a top-
down system imposed from above and hostile to all local and teacher
initiative.

This volume will help define, and clarify, objectives. It will also
serve to kick-start a nation-wide campaign.

Part 1:
Perspectives on Selection, Specialisation and Diversity

3

Has comprehensive education a future under New Labour?

Geoff Whitty

These have been tough times for comprehensive education, made all the harder by the recent loss of its most ardent advocate, Caroline Benn. We owe it to Caroline to continue the struggle to achieve her dream. One of Caroline's great strengths was the way in which she remained positive even when the going was rough. I am going to try to follow that example by attempting to identify some positive features in the present policy climate.

The development of comprehensive education goes beyond the issue of the struggle over comprehensive secondary schools, or selection at 11-plus, to embrace everything from nursery education to post-16 provision and beyond. In some of those fields, it is easier to identify progressive policies than it is on the more conventional terrain of comprehensive, non-selective secondary schooling, on which I shall concentrate here. But, although I will not be able to avoid the negative side of the balance sheet entirely, I will try to emphasise some of the spaces within which supporters of comprehensive schools can work.

The term 'comprehensive school' has never had an entirely un-ambiguous meaning. Sometimes it has meant having carefully balanced intakes, at other times taking all-comers from the local neighbourhood. Balance has sometimes meant academic balance, sometimes social balance. And there has never been agreement as to whether a single sex comprehensive school, or a denominational comprehensive school, is a contradiction in terms. When I was a teacher in a flagship comprehensive school in Crawley in the early 1970s, the debate was about whether we were aiming for merito-cratic or egalitarian comprehensives, and during its own history that particular school has fluctuated between the two models.

I think it is quite clear that, whatever some supporters of compre-hensive schools might want in the long term, certain definitions of a comprehensive school are not going to be on the official policy agenda in the short term, even if, as promised, New Labour's second term proves more radical than the first. New Labour believes in the meritocratic model of society and hence is looking to an education system to serve that aim. But, even within that, the extent of New Labour's commitment to comprehensive schools has sometimes been less than clear. There have even been some people close to New Labour arguing that it should formally rethink its opposition to academic selection, certainly at age 14 if not 11. Furthermore, al-though the vast majority of secondary schools are now compre-hensive at least in name, the continuing existence of selective schools leaves open the question of what precisely Labour now stands for in this respect. Gone is the firm conviction, as expressed by Ted Short back in the 1960s, that 'if it is wrong to select and segregate children... it must be wrong everywhere'.

The recent record on grammar schools has certainly not been en-couraging. Far from being an irrelevant sideshow, the issue is hugely significant in a number of local areas and its symbolic importance nationally remains immense. 'If there is no desire among local parents for a change in admissions policies, there will be no ballot and no change' said Labour in 1997 and that has remained the posi-tion. As we now know, the rules have made it virtually impossible to get a ballot in some areas and the Ripon experience of having a ballot has been decidedly dispiriting for supporters of compre-hensive schools. Nevertheless, there are still those actively seeking ballots and the issue will not be allowed to go away. On partial selection, the statutory position has been similarly unsatisfactory, although a few battles have been won courtesy of the Schools Adjudicator. It would, of course, be a great boost for the comprehensive schools movement if a second Blair government did act decisively to end selection at 11, but that is highly unlikely to happen. And, despite the continuing significance of formal selection, there are other policies that pose a potential threat to the future of comprehensive schooling that also need to be tackled.

In many respects, New Labour has continued and extended the previous government's espousal of diversity and choice in secondary education. Yet it became clear that, even last year, the Prime Minister still believed that most comprehensive schools were the same and havens of dull mediocrity at that. The government's enthusiasm for specialist schools has been partly a response to that belief. Although that policy, especially with an emphasis on specialist provision as a community resource, may seem to have something to commend it in principle in conditions of 'high' or 'post'modernity, it remains extremely difficult to deliver comprehensive schools in this country that are different but equal. The academic and social selection of children for unequal provision has long been the dominant principle on which secondary education has been organised. It is hardly surprising then that interest and aptitude in music, for example, are now being used by some schools to enhance the entry of academically able children from middle-class families at the expense of local children.

To me, as a sociologist as well as a socialist, New Labour's chosen path of fostering diverse forms of schooling within a broader commitment to comprehensive secondary education demands that serious attention be given to ways of preventing legitimate differences leading to unjustifiable inequalities. The danger of creating a hierarchy of schools based on the sorts of children who attend them is, of course, likely to be reinforced if there are significant differences in funding levels. We do not so far have research that is robust enough to tell us whether the recently heralded better performance of specialist schools results from anything other than their enhanced funding, but it will certainly make them increasingly attractive to some parents. With the numbers of specialist schools already capped in some areas, there will be a real danger of a two-tier system emerging.

However, this is not to argue against schools having distinctive characters. At times, supporters of comprehensive schools defend them by saying they are not uniform, while at the same time resisting more explicit attempts to let them develop distinctive characters. The comprehensive schools movement needs to clarify its position on this, but it is absolutely right to insist that specialist school status is not abused. This might have been easier if, rather than encouraging specialist schools as such, New Labour had taken a 'schools-within-schools' approach to maintaining a sense of commonality while recognising difference, as has been done to great effect in some North American cities.

Although probably not as damaging as first feared, the decision to have distinctions between 'community' and 'foundation' schools, alongside the longstanding voluntary status, has also been unhelpful. Even though most foundation schools identify themselves as comprehensive schools, they are more likely than community schools to have sixth forms, relatively high proportions of middle-class pupils, and correspondingly low proportions of working-class and black pupils. This can lead to differentiation on social grounds, and their different standing in relation to school organisation and admissions policies creates significant, and unnecessary, opportunities to perpetuate traditional patterns of segregation.

There may nevertheless be some scope for pushing the comprehensive schools agenda further during New Labour's second term. A major concern among those committed to Labour's social democratic ideals was that, despite its broader emphasis on social inclusion, some of the education policies that New Labour inherited from the Conservatives were effectively exclusionary. Quasi-markets had allowed advantaged schools and advantaged parents to maximise their advantages at the expense of the disadvantaged. New Labour's subsequent policies have introduced greater regulation into the education market. Some aspects of that re-regulation have been controversial to say the least. But there has been a welcome recognition that, even if low expectations are part of the problem, increased investment and support for schools in areas of multiple disadvantage are necessary if working class and minority ethnic pupils are to achieve more. The latest statistics seem to suggest that, as a result, the achievement gap may at last be closing – and supporters of comprehensive schooling should celebrate that.

Yet even if this proves to be a clear trend, rather than a blip, there is an urgent need to increase the relative rate of improvement at the bottom end and make sure it extends to all disadvantaged groups. For this to happen, there will need to be a much clearer demarcation of the difference between Labour and the Conservatives, whose own agenda is now clear. Their 'free schools' proposals will entail a shift from quasi-markets towards more full-blown marketisation and privatisation and growing inequalities of provision. Labour would do well not to try to compete on the ground of individual and institutional self-interest but, instead to rebuild the sense of a public education service involving collaboration between schools, communities and appropriate external partners. If, in Michael Barber's words, New Labour seeks to 'link its traditional concern with equality with a new recognition of diversity', then it now needs to re-emphasise the equality dimension. If New Labour is to realise its declared goal of 'high quality education for the many, rather than excellence for the few' by the end of a second term, then the standards agenda and the inclusion agenda will need to be brought together and the priorities within and between them clarified.

So how might the cause of comprehensive secondary provision be furthered in this context? First, even within the policy of diversity and specialist schools, it is important to insist on a comprehensive system of secondary education. To avoid diversity becoming a hierarchical two-tier system, all schools in an area will need to work together in the interests of optimum provision for all pupils. Genuine collegiality among schools would be much easier if they were all put on the same legal and budgetary footing, whatever private and voluntary sector partners were involved in their governance. There also needs to be much stronger regulation of a common admissions system to stamp out current abuses. Status, budgets and admissions should thus be key areas for further action.

Then the inclusion agenda can be used to insist on the importance of social mix in secondary education. John Marks has recently returned to his claims that academic standards have suffered in England as a result of comprehensivisation. When I co-authored a review of the evidence last year, we came to the conclusion that overall there was too little robust evidence on either side of the argument to come to a definitive judgement on this, although David Jesson's recent analyses will need to be considered in any future revision.[1] What our pamphlet did not make explicit enough in my view was that improvement in academic achievement is not the only, or necessarily the most important, justification for comprehensive schools. Comprehensive schools are even more important to the social inclusion agenda than to the standards agenda.

Anthony Giddens has pointed to the problem of self-exclusion at the top of British society as well as social exclusion at the bottom. The Excellence in Cities initiative may have the effect of retaining more middle class children in inner city state comprehensive schools, at the same time as raising achievement among the socially excluded, but it would be good to see Labour trying even harder to include all its citizens within the mainstream of public provision. Getting the balance right between the positive effects of 'critical mass' and the dangers of middle class colonisation of particular schools at the expense of working class families will be difficult, but a socially inclusive strategy is surely worth fighting for.

Then there are other aspects of inclusion that could be pursued in New Labour's second term. Education Action Zones have provided some examples of multi-agency working between education, health and welfare services to tackle multiple disadvantage. However, I suspect the New Community Schools initiative in Scotland, drawing on the experience of full-service schools in the USA, may well provide a better model for comprehensive school-based services and greater community involvement in schools. With greater emphasis on collaboration rather than competition between schools, there ought also to be scope for experimentation with new ways of addressing the democratic deficit in education through local education forums. Such arrangements would help the vital process of developing social capital in disadvantaged areas.

It is also surely time to pursue the question of the comprehensive curriculum, one of the key challenges for the comprehensive school identified by David Hargreaves in the 1980s. The government has indicated that secondary education will be a priority in its second term. At Key Stage 4, the issue still seems to be seen largely in terms of academic or vocational routes, or the balance between them, rather than an overall and inclusive reconceptualisation of the curriculum. But Key Stage 3 is likely to be a major priority where current thinking is rather less clear. Here, in my view, Labour should look to enrich rather than narrow the curriculum, while making it more challenging. Raising literacy and numeracy scores by gradgrindery, or by neglecting areas such as the arts, is not in anyone's long term interests, least of all the socially disadvantaged. Reforms in some countries have managed to tackle the unquestionable need to raise standards in the basics, without sacrificing breadth. Labour's introduction of education for citizenship into the national curriculum and various initiatives in personal and social education are part of the answer. But the next government will need to take things further, perhaps by picking up on some of David Hargreaves' recent ideas on encouraging creativity and innovation.[2]

Not surprisingly, teachers have rather similar needs. Labour governments of the 1960s and 1970s managed to harness the commitment and creativity of teachers for the comprehensive project. Even allowing for a bit of 'golden age-ism' in this view, the contrast with the present situation is certainly stark. This government has still to win the hearts and minds of teachers, except in so far as they fear the alternative even more. The formation of the General Teaching Council had considerable symbolic value for the teaching profession, while the resignation of Chris Woodhead from Ofsted certainly raised morale for a time. But there is still a long way to go before teachers feel that this government trusts and values their professionalism. Transferring some additional functions to the GTC would help, but the character and public image of teaching need serious attention. Although pay is a key factor in the current teacher supply crisis, too many people are put off teaching because it is seen as a bureaucratic rather than a creative profession. This, together with the attraction of the new media industries, may be one of the reasons for an unprecedented shortage of English teachers in some parts of London. As with pupils, incentives and rewards for creativity and innovation will need to be put back into the system and give teaching some of the excitement as well as the challenge that many of us felt when we started teaching in comprehensive schools in the 1960s.

In conclusion, I think we will have to accept that there is not just one model of comprehensive schooling and that contemporary societies demand greater degrees of diversity and choice than may have been the case in the past. New Labour's plans for diversity and choice within a broadly comprehensive system do not yet provide enough systemic safeguards to stop that becoming a selective system in all but name. But there are tensions within New Labour education policy. Those of us concerned with issues of equity and inclusion need to seize what opportunities we can. I have tried to suggest that, although the climate may be less than optimal for comprehensive schooling in the conventional sense, there are still important things we can do to take some of the principles of comprehensive secondary education forward. I am sure that is what Caroline Benn would have tried to do.

Notes

1. A conference paper by David Jesson suggesting that 'brighter pupils 'do better' at comprehensives' was reported in *The Times* on 2 November 1999. Some of the data is contained in Jesson, D. (2000) 'The comparative evaluation of GCSE value-added performance by type of school and LEA', which can be downloaded from http://www.york. ac.uk/depts/econ/rc/cperm.htm

2. These ideas were put forward in a talk David Hargreaves gave at the Institute of Education on 22 November 2000 on the theme 'Towards education for Innovation: how can education systems meet the demands of a knowledge society?', sponsored by the Design Council, *The Guardian* and Demos.

4
Selection by specialisation
Clyde Chitty

It is easy to be depressed about the Labour Government's policy towards education in general and towards comprehensive education in particular. But I am refusing to allow myself to be downcast, partly because last night I went to a concert at Goldsmiths College given by our PGCE secondary music students – and it was simply fantastic. It made me realise (if I actually needed reassurance) that whatever the Government does to make teaching difficult and unrewarding, there are still some marvellous people going into the profession, and I feel very proud to be at Goldsmiths and to be working with them. I just wish we had a government which shared that pride and did not come up with policies like 'performance-related pay' designed to split the profession and create damaging hierarchies in the staffroom.

Comprehensive education is clearly going through a difficult period at present, but before I outline the main problems as I see them, I want to say something about the fundamental beliefs that Caroline Benn and I believed ought to underpin the comprehensive reform.

For both Caroline and me, the whole point of comprehensive education has been to establish the concept of educability, the idea that *all* children have talents and abilities which are there to be fostered and developed by creative and committed teachers.

The divided secondary system of the post-war period was clearly based on a whole set of false assumptions, notably the idea that it was possible to say, from the results of mental tests applied at the age of ten or eleven, what a child's future accomplishments might be. And that doctrine has a pretty evil ancestry which can be traced back to the early decades of the 20th century. While I would not wish to argue that all those who believed in the efficacy of intelligence testing or in fixed innate ability were either eugenicists or racists, I think it can be demonstrated that the mental measurement movement had its origins in concerns about racial purity and mental degeneracy. It is surely no coincidence that a number of leading eugenicists and psychometrists were highly successful in securing positions of power in local authorities in the period before and after the First World War which enabled them to influence education and social policy: Raymond B. Cattell in Leicester; George Auden first as a member of the York School Board and then as School Medical Officer for Birmingham; Ellen Pinsent as a co-opted member of the Birmingham School Board; above all, Cyril Burt in London. It was Burt who did so much to establish psychometry as a pseudo-science and who was to become one of the chief begetters of the 11-plus examination which effectively destroyed the life-chances of generations of working-class children.

It was the fatalistic notions of the intelligence-testers that Caroline and I were most concerned about. We believed that the comprehensive reform has no meaning unless it challenges the fallacy of fixed ability or potential in education. It should aim to dismantle all the structures rooted in that fallacy that act as barriers to effective learning while, at the same time, it should facilitate practices that enable everyone to enjoy a full education. It is not concerned merely to offer opportunities to learn. It recognises and proclaims the right to benefit from the full range of learning that is available for each age group in the compulsory period of schooling – with a full choice of learning at the later stages of life.

The very last piece that Caroline and I wrote together was concerned with challenging the myth that 'educational potential is a fixed quantity' for a collection of papers on 'the future of democratic comprehensive education' edited by Bob O'Hagan and published in 1999 under the general title *Modern Educational Myths*. These papers were based on a series of popular lectures held in one or other of thirteen comprehensive schools in north-east Derbyshire during the Autumn Term 1997 and the Spring Term 1998. The lectures were advertised under the broad umbrella title *The Chesterfield Papers: Modern Educational Fallacies*.

Going back to when it all began and to the time when Caroline and I first met, the first piece we ever wrote together was in the late 1960s, and it was called 'Non-streaming in comprehensives' and published in the journal *Comprehensive Education* (number 12, Summer 1969, pp. 2-8). That was in the heady days following the publication (in July 1965) of Circular 10/65 when we really did think that the case for comprehensive schooling had been made and that the future was going to be very bright. The Comprehensive Schools Committee had been launched in the Autumn of 1965, and Caroline was our Information Officer, producing a detailed annual survey of the progress of the comprehensive school reform. Tuesdays and Fridays were CSC days; and while Tony Benn was a member of the Wilson Cabinet, we ran the campaign from his office in the basement of the Benn house in Notting Hill Gate.

Bliss was it in that dawn to be alive; and yet, thirty years later, I can't honestly say that we have achieved all that we set out to achieve. It is possible that we took too many things for granted and that we underestimated the strength of the forces ranged against us. But it is also true that comprehensive school campaigners themselves made mistakes and created too many hostages to fortune. We allowed the aims of the movement to be sidetracked, forgetting that the comprehensive school was all about *education* and concentrating instead on side issues like social equality and 'social mixing'. It may well be true that Holland Park Comprehensive in the 1960s, as described by Melissa Benn in her article 'Child of a dream' in the *Education Guardian* (30 January 2001) had 'a wonderful and extraordinary mix of class, nationality and religion'; but, for me, that is not central to the comprehensive school ideal. *Half Way There*, the major report on the British comprehensive school reform that Caroline co-authored with Brian Simon and which was first published in 1970, contains the classic statement: 'A comprehensive school is *not* a social experiment; it is an educational reform' (p. 64). In other words, it might be very exciting if a comprehensive school has a genuine 'social mix', but it is not a *sine qua non* of a school's success; what matters is developing the right teaching approaches to enable every child to succeed.

The first school that I taught in was Malory Comprehensive, a successful mixed comprehensive school with around 1,450 students serving a forty-year-old working-class housing estate on the out-skirts of Bromley. This was an exciting place to be part of in the late 1960s, with an impressive record of success in external examina-tions and a growing local and national reputation for the quality of its drama and music productions. The students I taught were bright, funny and, above all, remarkably easy to motivate. Looking back to that happy period of my life, I'm not sure anything would have been gained by drafting in middle-class children from other parts of Bromley to create an artificial 'social mix'.

Selection by specialisation

Bringing the comprehensive school story up-to-date, it seems fair to point out that New Labour inherited a very divided secondary system when it came to power in May 1997. Quite apart from the seven per cent of students being educated in the independent sector, there were all those students being catered for by over 160 grammar schools, around 1,000 grant-maintained schools (accounting for nearly one in five of all secondary school students), fifteen City Technology Colleges, and 181 schools with a specialist orientation, 30 catering for languages and 151 for technology.

Yet far from dealing with the problems posed by so much selection and diversification, New Labour has done nothing to secure the abolition of the existing grammar schools (even making it difficult for groups of local parents to activate a ballot) and has actually in-creased the number of specialist schools and colleges. It is planned that there will be 800-1,000 specialist schools in operation by September 2003 and 1,500 by September 2006, meaning that nearly half of all maintained secondary schools will become specialist schools over the next five years.

Until now, the specialisms have been confined to sport, arts and media, technology, languages and music, but the new Green Paper[1] announced the addition of three new categories: engineering; science; and business and enterprise. It also lifted the current restriction on the number of specialist schools in those education authorities where there is already a high proportion. Business and enterprise schools are to be expected to develop strong curriculum-business links and also to develop teaching strengths in business studies, financial literacy and enterprise-related vocational programmes. All specialist schools and colleges will receive a £100,000 capital grant plus £123 per student per year – a total of £225,000 for a school of 1,000 students; the other 50 per cent of schools will apparently get nothing.

As I have already said, New Labour did not invent the idea of specialist schools. As I will go on to show, they were very much the brainchild of the 1992-97 Major administration; but the Conservatives could hardly have imagined that incoming Labour ministers would not only enthusiastically embrace their project, but also extend it beyond recognition.

It was back in July 1992 that John Patten contributed a telling article to the *New Statesman and Society* in which he argued that Socialists must now come to terms with the concept of 'selection by specialisation'. This is what he wrote:

> Selection is not, and should not be, a great issue for the 1990s, as it was in the 1960s. The new S-word for all Socialists to come to terms with is, rather, 'Specialisation'. The fact is that different children excel at different things; it is foolish to ignore it, and some secondary schools may wish specifically to cater for these differences. Specialisation, underpinned by the National Curriculum, will be the answer for some – though not all – children, driven by aptitude and interest, as much as by ability (17 July 1992).

Ten days later, John Patten's 1992 White Paper, *Choice and Diversity*, vilified supporters of comprehensive education for believing that 'children are all basically the same' and that 'all local communities have essentially the same educational needs'. It announced the expansion of the Technology School Initiative (TSI) to encompass other areas of the school curriculum. The subsequent Specialist Schools Programme encouraged secondary schools to develop 'their own distinctive identity and expertise' in one or other of four 'specialist subject areas': technology; languages; sports; and arts.

It is this modest Programme which has now been 'relaunched' by New Labour with a vigour and enthusiasm of which John Patten would have been proud. But, as we all realise, the Programme, particularly in its expanded form, has a number of basic flaws. In the first place, specialist schools perpetuate selection by being allowed to select up to ten per cent of their students on the basis of 'aptitude' for the particular specialism on offer. Then again, the whole specialist schools project actually widens inequalities in secondary education by reducing opportunities and creating a two-tier school system. And, thirdly, even among the specialist schools themselves, there can be no such thing as parity of esteem. As the Socialist Teachers' Alliance Education Group has been keen to emphasise in a number of their pamphlets (see, for example, *Is Comprehensive Education Safe in New Labour's Hands?*, published in 1996), in a class-divided and competitive society, specialisms are never equal: they rapidly become ranked in a hierarchy of status. In other words, a *specialist* school is often a *selective* school; and at the top of the hierarchy will be those schools specialising in the sort of academic education which leads on to 'high-status' jobs. You might talk about 'aptitude' but that simply becomes a convenient 'code-word' for 'academic ability'; and the whole idea of specialist schools, the whole idea of perpetuating that form of diversification, is actually to *abandon* the comprehensive principle.

In a letter she wrote to Brian Simon shortly before her death, Caroline pointed out that New Labour will not be able to bring back eleven-plus selection and abandon the comprehensive school but it will be able to do considerable damage under the guise of modernisation.[2] This is the point we need to be constantly aware of. New Labour will work hard to ensure that there is both selection between schools and selection within schools. Ministers will continue to proclaim the merits of banding, streaming and setting and ignore the research carried out by Caroline and myself for *Thirty Years On*, and by Jo Boaler in the case of mathematics. We also know that David Blunkett is anxious that so-called 'less able' students should be steered into vocational paths at the age of 14 (see report in *The Guardian*, 24 January 2001).

It is a depressing note on which to end; but I would argue that there is now more actual selection in the education system of England and Wales than existed in the immediate post-war period. Whatever else you might say about the old 11-plus, it did at least have a *degree* of objectivity and fairness about it. It did enable *some* working-class children to get through to grammar school, whatever you might think about the sort of education a grammar school offered and however alienated working-class students might have felt in that type of school. The selection we have now is far more sophisticated, more hidden and in many ways, I think, more obscene. It is our task to make sure that people are aware of what is happening in the cause of 'modernisation' and 'progress'.

Conclusion

The Government cannot bring back the 11-plus and it cannot envisage the creation of large numbers of new secondary modern schools; but we have to be eternally vigilant in analysing the insidious ways in which selection is creeping back into the system and the comprehensive ideal is being subverted. If Caroline were here today, I am sure she would want to emphasise that the movement is still about establishing *genuine* comprehensive education, against the opposition of the New Labour government which dislikes it, hates it, just as much as did its Conservative predecessors. Tony Blair and David Blunkett may talk about 'modernising' the comprehensive principle; we must make sure that in the process, they don't achieve their objective of destroying it.

Notes

1. The Green Paper *Schools: Building on Success: Raising Standards, Promoting Diversity, Achieving Results* published on 12 February 2001.
2. This letter appeared in the Spring 2001 number of *Forum*

5

Promoting comprehensive education

Margaret Tulloch

Surely Labour supporters should be angry that after four years of a Labour Government with a massive majority as many children face the 11-plus examination as when Labour took office in 1997?

When it first took power this Government could have ended selection at a stroke. Instead it has rumbled on throughout its time in office. Essentially the Government's attitude to selection is a passive one. The School Standards and Framework Act requires that there should be no more selection on ability; the School Admissions Code of Practice sets out what would be fair admissions procedures, and Adjudicators can act if complaints are made.

Government has told us that ending selection is not part of the big picture – it is a side issue involving only a few schools – not relevant to the Government's agenda of raising standards and promoting social inclusion. We need to give the lie to that claim. This can be illustrated by examining the background to the government's legislation.

The manifesto upon which the Government was elected in May 1997 gave the following commitment on comprehensive education:

> *In education we reject both the idea of a return to the 11-plus and monolithic comprehensive schools that take no account of children's differing abilities. Instead we favour all-in schooling*

which identifies the distinct abilities of individual pupils and organises them into classes to maximise their progress in individual subjects. In this way we modernise the comprehensive principle, learning from the experience of its 30 years of application.....

The manifesto went on to say

Any changes in the admission policies of grammar schools will be decided by local parents.

The first consultation on regulations to implement the latter policy was announced in August 1997 – without a press release. Further, the consultation document was sent by the DfEE only to grammar schools and to LEAs with grammar schools. CASE and other organisations had to ask to see the document. We were told that the limited circulation was a Ministerial decision. It seemingly did not occur to the DfEE that primary and secondary modern schools are directly affected by the existence of selection at 11-plus, and so therefore deserved to be 'consulted'.

During the second, more detailed, consultation it was pointed out by several LEAs, for example, that the proposed feeder school ballot regulations would disenfranchise local parents. However virtually all objections made then and during subsequent passage of the Bill through Parliament were ignored. We know from conversations with the DfEE that beyond this 'consultation' they did no research about what would be the likely effects of enfranchising parents in a particular way.

Legislation was fully implemented by December 1998. Ending selection in the 36 English LEAs where it still exists would require 48 parental ballots of parents – ten area ballots where all parents would be able to vote and 36 ballots relating to groups of grammar schools or to single (stand alone) grammar schools where only parents whose children attend 'feeder' schools are entitled to vote. Feeder schools are those which have sent a total of five or more children to the grammar schools in question over the last three years. However before such ballots could take place, petitions have to be signed by one in five of the parental electorate. All these signatures would have to be collected during a petition year starting in September and ending in the following July.

What happened then?

During 1999 campaigns were set up in some of the areas where there are grammar schools – Ripon, Kent, Trafford, Sutton, Barnet, Birmingham, Buckinghamshire, Medway, and Kingston. The Bucks campaign still continues. These campaigns were set up in good faith, encouraged not by the legislation but because campaigners believed that they had to try to end selection and that if this was the only way, they would go for it.

CASE set up a specific campaign – Say NO to Selection – to campaign nationally for an end to selection and to support campaigners who wanted to set up local campaigns to end selection. An email newsletter was widely distributed. We have put campaigners in touch with each other and with the media and tried to bring about an informed debate.

What have we learnt?

It is just under a year since the Ripon ballot when members of Ripon CASE, people with values they thought the Labour Government shared, were left to take the full force of the tabloid press while Government looked the other way. All campaigners, I would say, have ended up cynical and angry with a Labour Government.

Had there not been a ballot in Ripon many people would still be unaware of the unfairness of the process. Both there and in Kent, Barnet, Birmingham and Trafford, campaigners have managed to make selection an important local issue. Further – in trying to make this legislation work, campaigns have illustrated how ridiculous the legislation is.

- In a feeder school ballot, only parents who send their children to feeder schools i.e. those which have sent a total of five or more pupils to the grammar school in question during the current year and the preceding two years, qualify to vote. As a result of this many parents living near a grammar school which, if it were comprehensive, would be their neighbourhood school, are not able to sign the petition or vote. For example, parents whose children attend infant schools or small schools do not get a vote. Parents whose children attend a nursery unit attached to primary school will get a vote while those who attend stand alone nursery units will not. Parents who send their children to private schools (as in Ripon) are inevitably over represented as prep schools often send children to grammar schools.

- Campaigners find it difficult to obtain parental lists as only parents from the school concerned in the ballot can ask for them. Moreover these lists may be inaccurate as parents may move without telling the school. Trafford campaigners found some addressees to be grandparents.

- Schools are required to send information to the Electoral Reform services. But they are often slow to do so, so campaigners cannot reach the threshold required. It took five months for the threshold number for the Bucks campaign (18,453) to be calculated. And feeder school campaigns can't even start before these schools have been identified. Further, information about the feeder schools may be inaccurate.

- Petition signatures can't be carried over from one petition period to another, despite that fact that only part of one cohort of parents will become ineligible each year and a new one eligible. In other words the legislation assumes parents will change their minds about wanting a ballot from one year to the next.

- Petition forms cannot be sent out through pupil post as the DfEE rules that this might be interpreted as the school taking sides.

- Collecting signatures door to door is hugely time-consuming. The petition itself takes ages to fill in. Signatures may be difficult for the Electoral Reform Services to validate because people are not always sure of the name of their children's school.

- In area ballots, parents who live in a selective areas but send their children out of the LEA, most likely for comprehensive education, have to register to sign the petition and vote, whereas parents living outside the area and sending their children to grammar schools in the LEA are automatically registered. Campaigners can't get lists of these parents so have to stand around at bus stops hoping to encourage them to register and then collect their signatures.

- There are seemingly arbitrarily huge differences in the number of signatures to trigger a ballot. For instance about 600 were needed to get a ballot over one grammar school in Ripon whereas Bucks required about 1500 signatures per grammar school and Barnet about 2000 per grammar school.

- This should be contrasted with the fact that only ten signatures are needed on a letter to the Electoral Reform Services to trigger the requirement that it collects the information to assemble the list of feeder schools and establish the threshold number. This process costs a great deal of public money. In contrast, we see that thousands of signatures are needed before parents can even be asked if they want change.

- There is no limit on spending: Ripon proselectionists could afford to send a video to every home. Since the Ripon ballot minor changes introduced by Estelle Morris allow each 'side' to send out an A4 leaflet via the schools. But this applies only if a ballot is triggered. Misinformation and unfair practices emerge long before that, as soon as a campaign starts.

- Campaigns are long drawn out and complicated. Campaigners are forced to focus on getting signatures when the real issue is ending selection. Exhausted by the time the ballot comes, campaigners found the ballot papers were returned before they had time to campaign and then they had a long wait for the result.

- All campaigns need people willing to devote a great deal of their time. This is difficult in any circumstances but campaigners to end selection have found they need the hide of a rhinoceros to cope with the vilification by the local and national press.

But what is by far the worst feature of the whole of this ridiculous consequence of the legislation is that parents are given no proper information upon which to decide. It is surely irresponsible of Government to say parents should decide and then set up a system which does not ensure informed debate. As a result of this, proselectionists get away with defending the *status quo*. The talk is of abolition, excellence and choice and 'better the devil you know'. Children and their rights and the effect of selection do not get much of a look-in. Most professionals such as teachers and LEA officers do not make their views clear. There are no plans for parents to decide upon so debate is stifled and this means that parents are voting in a vacuum. Parents should have to vote on a principle. In fact it is encouraging that as many as a third of Ripon parents voted to end selection, on principle, having no idea what this might mean in terms of local school reorganisation.

Contrast this with the situation in Guernsey and Northern Ireland where elected local government is consulting local people and informing local debate.

So where do we go from here?

Selection is too important an issue to be left to the chance of a local campaign needing to collect signatures before anything can change. Retaining selection directly affects the Government's policy of raising standards and creating a more inclusive education system. If, as research seems to show, comprehensive systems do just as well academically as selective systems, is this not an argument for ending a system which tells three quarters of $10^{1}/_{2}$ year olds that they have failed? Why demotivate young children like this?

The Government is wrong to claim that selection affects only a small area and a small number of children and is therefore peripheral to the main agenda. There are only 164 grammar schools but if you add to that the number of secondary moderns notionally created, nearly 20% out of about three and half thousand English secondary schools are directly affected by selection to grammar schools.

Ending selection is entirely in line with the Government's stated aim's – it is not a side issue. For example, the mission statement of the DfEE is:

> *To give everyone the chance through education, training and work to realise their full potential and thus build an inclusive and fair society and a competitive economy.*

Delegates at the Labour Party conference last September voted *for secondary schools which build the confidence and self esteem of all our children.*

What's to be done?

- The Government, under existing regulations, could encourage grammar school governing bodies to change to comprehensive admission policies now.

- It could challenge the Tory-established policy that schools should be able to become grammar schools

- It could champion comprehensive education and highlight its achievements.instead of using terms such as monolithic, one-size-fits-all, and even 'bog-standard' schools. It is fond of saying 'what matters is what works' and yet seems unable to accept that this applies to comprehensive education.

- I believe it unlikely that a future Labour government would drop the requirement for a ballot of parents but it could be done very differently. Perhaps only parents of the children in the primary schools should have the vote.

- CASE believes new legislation is needed to end the requirement for a petition before a ballot. A minimum turnout in a ballot is enough to ensure that there is sufficient support for change.

- A new Labour Government should require LEAs or school organisation committees to bring forward specific proposals to end selection by test at 11. These proposals should be discussed locally. Professionals should be encouraged to give their views. Government should encourage change. This could then be followed by a ballot of all the parents in the area. The area defined could be the whole LEA or one within the LEA in what might be the catchment area of the particular schools. But it is crucial that parents be informed about selection. They need to be clear about what a vote for change might mean. Plans should be detailed. Funds must be promised. I think this would have the support of many grammar school heads because they would at least know where they were.

What to do

- Join CASE to campaign for comprehensive education.

- Challenge the idea that selection is a side issue, irrelevant to standards and social inclusion.

- The Government is not minded to change the legislation so supporters of comprehensive education have to persuade them.

- A general election offers a real opportunity for change. Supporters of comprehensive education should write to all the candidates urging them to end selection. Send CASE the replies you receive.

- Once the election is over we must lobby for change. We need a Government which champions comprehensive education and recognises its achievements.

6

A Comprehensive Agenda?

Carole Regan

If you want to know what New Labour thinks about education you only have to look at what they are doing to and about teachers. There's a crisis in teacher recruitment and retention. The vacancy rate is growing – 10% in my own area, Tower Hamlets, and turnover rate between 10 and 20% in some London boroughs. People talk about it being like the staff shortages in the 1980s. But it's much worse. In the 80s we didn't have the National Curriculum, league tables and a pile of 'initiatives': Performance Management, Threshold, PRP, OFSTED – but we did have publicly funded and accountable Local Education Authorities and we had the ILEA! This crisis is qualitatively different.

The Government response is denial that there's a crisis, and a pay settlement which, at 3.67% is an insult. On radio recently, the Education Secretary included the threshold payment of £2000 as part of the pay deal. He said newly qualified teachers were going to get a massive increase of £1000. He also said we could all get onto the superteacher (ASTs) scale, forgetting to mention that there are not many people who can do so and even less who want to.

All these wonderful offers, are according to the Government, going to solve the recruitment crisis. Anyone who believes that probably believes that teachers are happy and content and that New Labour is supportive of comprehensive education. The truth is that teachers are poorly paid and the job is no longer enjoyable. Teachers are demoralised and looking for escape routes.

The treatment of teachers by New Labour is a reflection of their attitude towards education, and in particular comprehensive education, from the primary schools to Further and Higher Education. Comprehensive education is certainly not

- the Private Finance Initiative (PFI)
- action zones
- beacon schools
- specialist schools
- City Academies
- Fresh Start
- foundation schools
- Excellence in Cities
- vocational education based on the needs of the city and industry
- league tables – baseline testing, CATS, SATs, or
- naming and shaming

For those who are not sure what many of these institutions are:

Beacon Schools are the so-called best schools in the area, which we are all supposed to emulate, but which we can't because every parent wants to send their child to that school, so rendering all the other schools second choice. So the students who fail to get their 'choice' end up going to schools they wanted to avoid.

Specialist Schools are schools which 'specialise' in a particular area, like ICT, Performing Arts, etc and select on the basis of ability to do the specialism.

City Academies are inner city schools whose objectives and procedures are so far uncertain

Excellence in Cities is a crude attempt to appease middle class parents at the expense of the rest. The gifted and talented (GATs) students get to go on trips, attend special classes to make sure they succeed. In the words of a recent document I received from our GAT coordinator: 'Don't give them more – give them better'. This raises the question of what the vast majority get – is it less? For the challenging students we have mentors – soon there will be more mentors than teachers. And why be a teacher when mentors receive £22,000 and newly qualified teachers £17,000? Don't get me wrong, I think mentors are valuable in assisting to motivate students to achieve their full potential. I just think that mentors should be for all, not just the few.

If my experience is anything to go by, the school students who don't earn the GAT tag just become cynical and disaffected. The 'Gifted and Talented' don't want to be singled out either. Comments from students that I've heard: 'How come they're going to the London Eye?', 'It's something to do with being clever isn't it?', 'Yea I was chosen for that but I said I didn't want to go.'

The Private Finance Initiative and outsourcing produces the same result, whether it's selling off the school's support services, maintenance contracts, or cleaning contracts with 25 year to run – an end to the state education system and any idea of comprehensive education. There's no way we can defend comprehensive education without defeating privatisation. There have been some notable victories in the campaign against privatisation – Pimlico School, Haringey, various individual schools. We must extend and build on these successes.

Last week we had another of New Labour's big new ideas: more Vocational education. I supported GNVQs because they gave those students who didn't acquire the required A levels to gain enough qualifications to enter college or university through an alternative route. Now, with Curriculum 2000, the new GNVQ examinations have been made more academic and scarcely different from GCE A levels. It is wrong to believe that education should be tailored to the so-called demands of industry. What vocational courses could be offered to students in South Wales, where the steel works are about to close – leisure and tourism? My own experience at a secondary modern school in Manchester was that the girls were told that their futures would lie in the mills and the boys that theirs lay in engineering, and then what happened? Mills and engineering factories shut. We don't want to go back to those bad days of tripartite education which damaged the majority of students.

This government constantly talks about how it is 'standards not structures' that make a difference, although their record would indicate that they are using structures to implement a standards agenda which is seriously threatening comprehensive education. Caroline Benn and Clyde Chitty, in their book *Thirty Years On,* argued cogently that structures are central to successful education and that the structures needed involve the provision of state funded comprehensive education. There are students, parents, teachers and governors who are still resisting the implementation of selection, from streaming within schools to other forms of entry selection.

Finally, little is said by the Labour government about questions of equality in the areas of race, gender and class. These are issues which we need to bring to the fore as a means of defending the comprehensive system. This book is a step towards reasserting these principles.

7
The Community School
Geoff Carr

ommunity schooling provides the means for the comprehensive school to address the social inclusion agenda. It
further develops the concept of the comprehensive school by
integrating the educational experience of the school with that of its
immediate and wider community on a reciprocal basis, by giving as
much as it receives, by serving the community and being served by
the community. By giving, for instance, individual community
members the chance to develop self-confidence through educational, social and/or other achievements, community schooling
enables them to further their own objectives but also, crucially, to
work within their communities to achieve forms of collective learning as a prelude to the empowerment and change of that community.
Thus, community education is both personal and political.

An Adult Perspective
Adult Learning, for example, where adults follow GCSE, GNVQ or
A Level lessons, alongside school students free of charge, is especially helpful to those who are tentative about committing themselves to a full-scale learning programme. Once they have achieved
modest successes in school, adult learners often feel confident
enough to enrol on local college courses or to tackle more challenging and satisfying career paths. There are other less predictable
benefits from such schemes, too. The presence of adults within
classes enriches the curriculum for all students by bringing an adult
viewpoint to subjects or key issues. Consider, for instance, the per-

spective brought to a GNVQ Health and Social Care lesson by a young (or even not so young) Adult Learning mother. And, as the value of this perspective is acknowledged in class by teacher and students, self-esteem on the part of the learner begins to rise. Such precious interactions can occur across the academic and vocational curriculum of the community comprehensive school. Local historical knowledge, particularly that provided by third-age learners, can greatly enrich learning in, for instance, Humanities lessons, at the same time breaking down unnecessary and unhelpful barriers between young and old. By regularly inviting members of the local community of all ages and walks of life into school, to participate in the teaching and learning process, most of the damaging myths about 21st century comprehensive education can be demolished in a single morning. Best of all though, community schooling is a golden opportunity to identify, celebrate and further develop the multitude of talents, wisdom and hitherto unrecognised skills that are far too often lying dormant within every community.

The School at the centre of the community

An active and dynamically-led community school can bring cohesion to a community by becoming the centre-point for a wide array of services on which the local community depends. One-stop shops, providing contact (and a focal point) with social services, housing support groups, youth services, health advice etc., all have a logical home in the school, which is often already at or near the centre of the community. School students benefit too by gaining easy access to these services e.g. a Health Centre which doubles as a drop-in family planning advice centre for teenagers. Imaginative approaches to the use of the school site, such as weekend, evening and school holiday opening, facilitate the widest possible range of broader learning opportunities such as summer schools for children and opportunities for community members to acquire skills, knowledge, information and advice which will help to improve their employment prospects, increase community involvement and create a context for positive social contact.

Listening to the voices of the students

The extent to which a school takes seriously the point of view of its students also plays a crucial role within the development of community schooling. Once a school Student Council breaks away from repetitious, unrewarding debates about school dinners or uniform, it can become involved in school management, policy development, lesson planning and other crucial elements of school life such as the appointment of staff. The benefits of developing the student voice in these ways are soon apparent. If students have helped create the school's discipline code, they are more likely to adhere to it. This is equally true of partnerships made outside the school.

One of the most depressing trends of recent years has been the large-scale disengagement of young people from politics at both local and national level. Perhaps the habit of suppressing the views of young people both in and out of school has contributed to the lack of involvement in local and national democratic processes. By involving young people in the democratic process through such initiatives as student councils, local youth forums or the national youth parliament, they will almost inevitably become more committed to its survival and growth.

Increased democracy in school provides young people with the knowledge, skills and the incentive to become committed, participative and politically astute citizens who are much more likely to contribute to the remaking and enrichment of their communities than those with no such experience. Within the community schooling context, the comprehensive school student has, therefore, the potential to become an agent of individual, educational and societal change – and in doing so the community school liberates the student and empowers the community.

All schools are community schools?

It is not true that all schools are automatically community schools just because they exist within a community. A community school acknowledges and builds upon its role as a microcosm of the community within which it finds itself. It recognises that its interests are intricately caught up with those of its community. It follows logically, therefore, that in working with the community to identify and serve its needs and in helping the community to become a truly learning community, one that is fully equipped to face the turbulence of constant change, the school will also become strongly identified with and share in subsequent community successes.

8

Selection under New Labour: the case of the inner cities

Rachel Jones

New Labour's standards agenda is at its most intense in the inner cities. Policies that are being promoted in inner city secondary schools are related to New Labour's desire to raise educational attainment in order to guarantee 'employability' in a globalised economy over which, they argue, they now have little control. Increasing differentiation both within and between schools is seen as not only uncontroversial but desirable. Alongside this, New Labour has a further objective in preventing the emergence of what they see as an urban 'underclass'. They are well aware of how the effects of market forces and the absence of welfare provision have led to highly volatile situations in American cities like Los Angeles.

While concerns are mounting about rural working class unemployment, notions of 'social exclusion' generally centre on the decay of the inner cities: urban unemployment, petty crime, substance abuse, teenage pregnancy and non-participation in civic activities. Paranoid about increasing divisions in urban areas, New Labour also seeks to make urban education 'acceptable' to the middle classes in order to retain at least some 'social mixing'. Labour promotes this agenda as 'socially progressive': for example, in the *Excellence in Cities Newsletter* of March 1999, David Blunkett and Tony Blair proclaim:

> *Standards have been too low for too long...we need to tackle the problems of failure and low aspirations in the cities more*

directly; and we need a sharp early improvement in parental confidence in the capacity of city schools to cater for ambitious and high achieving pupils.

Launched in September 1999, *Excellence in Cities* (EiC) has become a Labour flagship. Its key strands are: 'Gifted and Talented' children, Learning Support Units, Learning Mentors, Specialist Schools, Beacon Schools, City Learning Centres and mini Education Action Zones.

The Gifted and Talented strand caters for 5-10% of the 'highest attaining' students and provides them with significant additional funding and provision, while demanding that they should experience a significantly differentiated curriculum. While in many schools this will be provided through setting, it can be anticipated that a completely separate 'fast track' stream will increasingly be introduced. This is particularly likely given that targets have to be set for early GCSE entry in multiple subjects, which will be hard to achieve unless this group is timetabled separately.

Learning Support Units and Learning Mentors are aimed at students with 'barriers to learning' or 'at risk of exclusion'. Working not just with students but also through home visits, targets are set for attainment, attendance and behaviour. Where students are deemed too disruptive to participate in regular class groups they may periodically be withdrawn and then reintegrated. (Such intervention and increasing emphasis on parental responsibility for student participation in schooling is further emphasised and extended in the recent Green Paper *Building on Success* (DfEE, 2001).)

Beacon Schools are deemed to be 'good schools' as a result of nomination by Ofsted or because of high exam results. EiC also includes four categories of Specialist School – Technology/Expressive Arts/Language/Sports colleges, with significant extra funding (£1/4 to 1/2 million from *per capita* and matched funding in the first year) and some curricular deregulation to permit specialisation. (Again proposals to extend this are outlined in *Building on Success*, with the addition of further types of specialist schools.)

City Learning Centres (CLCs) are designed to promote on-line learning and develop a community learning focus. They are posed within a construct of a 'learning society', providing access to courses for the wider community, not just school children. The longer-term vision of CLCs is as the hub of a wheel, with other schools and local institutions (for example, libraries) as spokes. Learners will be able to log on from a range of different institutions at different times to pursue studies.

But what does *Excellence in Cities* add up to in the standards and social inclusion/exclusion debate? Firstly, it provides a highly diversified system of existing schools. The retention of open enrolment is further legitimated through the provision of specialised schools, yet which kinds of families will prefer their child to go to a language rather than a sports college? Which families will try to place their child in a Beacon school? Ironically, this has echoes of the 'Choice and Diversity' agenda of the last Conservative government.

Taken to its logical conclusion, a combination of the *Excellence in Cities* initiatives may well lead not just to increased differentiation but to quite separate and tiered pathways. Extending ICT provision through the National Grid for Learning (NGfL) together with CLC on-line learning provides a model of education for a majority of students which is heavily reliant on ICT, facilitated by learning support assistants and with some specialist teaching. While it can be argued that there are many positive aspects to this, it also has to be viewed, perhaps cynically, within the context of an acute teacher shortage. 'Gifted' and 'talented' students are likely to be provided with a quite separate programme involving more specialist teacher input. Students with 'barriers to learning' will migrate between Learning Support Units and the mainstream, depending on their meeting of targets.

This division of students into streams is exacerbated by a public examination system featuring tiered papers that are increasingly difficult to co-teach and has already led to significant numbers of schools moving to setting. This is reinforced further in the revision of Key Stage Four to permit students to drop areas in order either to specialise, to raise attainment in core subjects or else *in extremis* to participate in extended work related placements.

While *Excellence in Cities* is posed as a strategy for raising standards in inner city schools, its targets do not relate to the majority of students. Targets are set only for the highest attainers, and for those who often gain few if any formal qualifications at the end of compulsory schooling. It should be seen, then, as an intervention into the social exclusion debate rather than as a 'solution' to the standards agenda. It provides a response to the concerned middle classes who, while broadly supportive of State education, are fearful that their children might suffer from classroom disruption, and offers them the carrot of the Gifted and Talented strand. It also provides sustained intervention into the education and indeed the lives of disaffected students from socially 'non-compliant' families. What it never even begins to address is the root of this disaffection.

9

'School was not invented just for the little people to become the same as the big people'

Mike Davies

The chapter heading comes from Judith, a 13 year old student, quoted by Edward Blishen (p.30) in a wonderful book, *The school that I'd like,* published in 1969. The *Observer* newspaper had launched a project in the form of a competition which invited young people to contribute essays on how we might go forward and improve our schools. In his introduction to the resulting book Blishen (1969) writes an overview of the students' comments and finds what he calls

> ... a most striking coincidence of opinion. Standing out above everything else is the children's desire to teach themselves, rather than to be the passive targets of teaching; a great restlessness about classrooms, timetables, and the immemorial and so often inert routine of schools. The children seem to sense what their elders are slow to sense, that you enter the world....ill armed if all you have done is to submit, to some degree or other, to a pre-determined, pinched, examination-harried course of instruction, from which by its nature most of the excitement and surprise of learning are excluded.... They want to learn to govern themselves. They want to take risks... intellectually and emotionally'. (p.13/14).

You might wonder what happened in the thirty-four years since *The Observer* launched its competition? Have we all been asleep?

Interestingly we shall soon find out, as the *Guardian* (Birkett, 2001) newspaper is currently re-running the competition. It will be fascinating to read the results but, for now, a suspicion looms that while we skilfully re-arrange the deckchairs we allow many young people to sink.

I propose to focus on the experience of comprehensive education inside school and suggest some ways of moving forward, rather than dwelling on the appalling consequences for children and community that comes from our abdication to, and reliance on, the market to decide who goes to which school, unless of course you know how to work the system! Back inside the classroom....

Some recent research by colleagues at Kings College, London (Reay and Wiliam, 1999) into the impact tests have on the perception children hold of themselves suggests that the thirty-four years between competitions have brought very little change to schooling as experienced by children. The major impact of the 1988 Education Act seems to have been successfully to reinforce much that Edward Blishen's children found unwelcome in our schools. As an example, the researchers captured some conversation between children which illustrates the impact of National Curriculum assessment on students' definitions of themselves as learners:

Hannah: I'm really scared about the SATs (standard assessment tasks). Mrs O'Brien (a teacher at the school) came and talked to us about our spelling and David (the class teacher) is giving us times tables tests every morning and I'm hopeless at times tables, so I'm frightened I'll do the SATs and I'll be a nothing.

Dianne: I don't understand, Hannah. You can't be a nothing.

Hannah: Yea, you can 'cause you have to get a level like a level 4 or a level 5 and if you're no good at spellings and times tables you don't get those levels and so you're a nothing.

Dianne: I'm sure that's not right.

Hannah: Yes it is 'cause that's what Mrs O'Brien was saying.

What is fascinating about this conversation between two 10 year olds girls is how they define academic success as correct spelling and knowing your times tables. Yet the research team tell us that Hannah is an accomplished writer, a gifted dancer and artist and that she is good at problem solving. Yet none of these skills makes her somebody in her own eyes. Instead she sees herself as a failure, as an academic non-person, defined entirely in terms of the level to which her performance in the SATs is ascribed.

It is the corrosive effect of defining people through levels and numbers, and the glass ceiling this can impose on human dignity and development that I see as one of the main challenges to comprehensive education right now. We must never forget that all we do, all we plan and are involved in, is a manifestation of a set of values and beliefs, a view of the future and an anticipation of the role of the citizen within society. To reinforce and strengthen comprehensive education is to go beyond technical efficiency and recognise that many are currently on a path to emotional bankruptcy and a diminution of what we recognise and value as success. Future generations will pay a price for the current nonsenses with their perpetuation of selection and control. I can't place the quotation, but these approaches are wonderfully summed up by the person who wrote of the stupidity of someone measuring a mouth, contorting it in every possible way and measuring the various angles in an attempt to capture the warmth and glow of a smile. I guess painting by numbers has its limitations and so does our current preoccupation with pretending we can capture the gifts and talents of a person by levels and then calculate the added value by remeasuring them in twelve months time.

Elsewhere in the world there are different models that embody quite different conceptions of society and learning. Denmark, for example, has a proud tradition of Folk high schools with a particular emphasis on community involvement and participation; it shares with other Scandinavian countries a suspicion of external examinations and prefers a cooperative, mixed ability framework in which it is the responsibility of the whole class to ensure that all succeed. This is reinforced by the class staying with one teacher for virtually the whole curriculum right through to 16.

The lessening of the strait jacket that the subject-dominated curriculum can become is echoed in some other recent curriculum frameworks coming from South Africa and Hong Kong. Both are moving fast to implement proposals that see a curriculum underpinned and planned around a series of competences and attributes rather than subject content. In this country similar ideas are being proposed and developed by the Royal Society of Arts and are outlined their booklet *Opening Minds* (Bayliss, 1999).

Developments such as these are not isolated *ad hoc* ideas. Taken together, they begin to represent a very different conception of learning and learners. They offer totally new possibilities, schools fit for adolescents, person centred and respectful of the diversity of people not of the choice of systems.

Partly as a response to growing alienation and discord, many of these ideas have been brought together in a rapidly growing movement in the USA, the Coalition of Essential Schools (Sizer 1992). The Coalition is an umbrella organisation with member schools subscribing to a number of special features. Many echo the aspirations the Human Scale Education Movement has in this country. Among them are:

- a determination to personalising teaching and learning through a commitment that no teacher should have responsibility for more than 80 students in any one week; this supported through the creation of small teams of teachers who spend 'extended' periods of time with a group of students.

- practicing the guiding metaphor of student-as-worker rather than teacher as deliverer of information. There is much team teaching, with emphasis on the interconnectedness of knowledge and investigation of current and controversial issues of contemporary life.

- a growing practice of students celebrating their achievements through a series of exhibitions of their work, and of success being gauged in terms of the individual's own progress, often as part of a cooperative group.

- Other features of Coalition schools include teachers seeing themselves as generalists first and specialists second; involving parents and other community members as partners in shaping and engaging in the curriculum; allowing flexibility in the timetable so that time can be used as appropriate to task and activity and not preset and totally fixed a year in advance.

• Many Coalition Schools are also part of the growing move in the United States toward the establishment of Full Service Schools, with a deliberate strategy of promoting the school as a multi-agency centre of community support and regeneration. Scotland is pioneering a similar strategy of social inclusion through its New Community Schools programme.

This commitment to restructuring schools by breaking down the old nineteenth century factory model and developing centres of learning on a human scale is not new. I recall in the early 1980s reading an article by John Watts (1980), then Principal of Countesthorpe Community College in Leicestershire, in which he described how in Auckland, New Zealand a school had opened up totally new opportunities and choice for young people and their parents by federating into sub-units, a dreadful phrase for something that has so much potential.

The school had restructured into four or five units, each with a distinct ethos and commitment, ranging from one that was tightly defined by streaming and subject boundaries to one with an emphasis on enquiry work and class projects in a mixed ability context. What is important in light of today's mantra of 'choice and diversity' is that here was real choice, choice beyond the colour of the uniforms and numbers of computers per pupil, an opportunity for students with their parents, to join a school that sought to work with them and respect their differences and needs as persons. Interestingly, what is really significant is that Watts reported that over time the drift of parental choice was into what might be termed the 'progressive' unit.

Where is there such a possibility in the UK right now? Why do we deny parents such opportunities? Given all we know about multiple intelligences and the different learning styles that are represented within us all, how have we swallowed the 'one size fits all' central direction of so much that now defines the reality of students and teachers at school?

In the mid 1980s John Wilkins and I, as Co-Directors of Stantonbury Campus, Milton Keynes, moved to federate our schools into five Halls of roughly five hundred students each, instead of one gigantic school of two thousand, five hundred. The restructuring was part of a deliberate attempt to meet our aspirations that school should be a place where everyone was known well and there was a direct personal relationship with the parents; where relationships were taken as the fundamental cornerstone of our success; where relatively small teams of teachers worked across the curriculum with a relatively small cohort of students; where we matched the team structures with the geography of the site so that young people on transfer from primary did not wander a huge anonymous campus but had a stable base for much of their curriculum. This stability was not an end in itself but a springboard for staff and students to be creative, take risks, be challenged as well as supported, work in the community, enjoy residentials as well as study in the classroom – all alongside an absolute commitment to basic skills. All this would be so much easier today if we harnessed the potential of ICT, schools don't need to be anonymous warehouses any more.

Let me cut through this journey down rose-petaled memory lane and offer a framework for a stronger future for comprehensive education, I think that we need to look at:

- the way we can use time more flexibly and creatively;

- the possibilities of small teams working with a dedicated cohort of students across areas of the curriculum

- the new opportunities for independent work and work in depth that ICT gives us and the ending of the monopoly by the classroom teacher as sole information provider

- the organisation and structures that best foster supportive but challenging relationships

- the importance of promoting a sense of belonging through the careful use of physical space

- the implications of new insights into intelligences and learning styles for the way we organise students into groups

- the need for students to be partners in shaping at least part of their learning and to be engaged in problem based learning within the world they experience as well as beyond

- the need to make work meaningful, worthwhile and relevant to the learners, and that applies to assessment as well.

If we fail to embrace the future and continue the recipes of the past then, as Maureen O'Connor, who was the first editor the *Education Guardian*, wrote a decade ago: '...there is a real danger that secondary schools will gain the National Curriculum and much else, and lose their soul. What price standards then?' (O'Connor 1990).

References

Bayliss, Valerie (1999) *Opening Minds*, London: Royal Society of Arts

Birkett, Dea (2001) 'The school I'd like', *The Guardian*, 16 Jan.

Blishen, Edward (1969) *The School that I'd Like,* Harmondsworth: Penguin

O'Connor, Maureen (1990) *Secondary Education*, London: Cassell

Reay, Diane and Wilam, Dylan (1999) 'I'll be a nothing: structure, agency and the construction of identity through assessment', *British Educational Research Journal*, Vol.25, No3,)

Sizer, Theodore (1992) *Horace's School: redesigning the American High School*, New York: Houghton Mifflin

Watts, John (1980) *Towards An Open School*, London: Longman

10

Post-16 Education

Jon Duveen and Philippe Harari

Within our current system, the older the students become, the less comprehensive is their education. At the 16-19 level, for example, students are faced with a wide range of different institutions offering different kinds of courses. These different institutions do not work together to offer coherent educational provision. Instead, each institution stands alone in competition with others, each has its own corporate identity and is run as a business which needs to break even, rather than as a public service. This means that different institutions and different courses/qualifications do not enjoy parity of esteem; A levels seems to be generally considered more worthwhile than GNVQs, for example.

True comprehensive education in this sector is further undermined by an obsession with academic qualifications that stems from our universities and trickles down to infect the whole educational system. The post-16 sector is built upon a system of competition and selection; there does not seem to be anywhere in the country where even lip service is paid to comprehensive provision for post-16 students.

It is useful to consider what a truly comprehensive post-16 sector would look like. At the higher education level, we are so far from this ideal that it is difficult even to imagine comprehensive universities; but if non-selective comprehensive education is best for primary and secondary school children, why should university students be denied its benefits? In a primary or secondary school the debate may be about whether classrooms should be non-selective, but it is hard to imagine how non-selective classes would work post-16. However, non-selective colleges *are* possible and comprehensive post-16 education would allow all students to learn within the same coherent system, following a range of courses commanding equal levels of respect. An A level course is different from an intermediate GNVQ course, but it is not better.

A vision of a comprehensive 16-19 sector can be set out by considering what its curriculum might consist of, and how it would be planned and managed:

Curriculum

The Government introduced a series of changes to the A level and Advanced GNVQ systems in 2000. Collectively these changes were called Curriculum 2000. They broke the old A level courses into two separate courses, an initial AS course and an advanced A2 course. Students were expected to study four ASs, or possibly five, in their first year post 16 and three A2s in their second year. In addition the changes made the Advanced GNVQ more closely follow the model of the AS/A2 courses. The third change ensured that all AS/A2 and GNVQ students were able to enter for Key Skills qualifications.

The changes brought about by Curriculum 2000 have proved to be a lost opportunity for major reform of the post-16 qualification system. Although touted as being so, these changes are in reality extremely limited. The main reason for this is the Government's refusal to make any significant change to the 'gold standard' of the A level. With this as a fixed position there is limited scope for reform. For most level 3 students the adding of one extra subject at AS level does not significantly broaden their learning, although it does increase the time they have to attend college or school. This has a consequent effect on the time they have available for other things: homework, earning money, child care, let alone enjoyment.

One of the rationales that was offered for these changes was that it would allow subject content to be examined and where necessary reduced. Most areas show little or no reduction in content for AS and A2 and in some areas there has been an actual increase in content. The fact that teaching time has been reduced by about half a term, because students now have to sit exams at the end of AS and A2 in all their subjects, means that teaching time is squeezed with a consequent effect on those students who need support.

Another rationale for the introduction of Curriculum 2000 was that it would allow students on AS/A2 courses to take units from other qualifications, e.g. Advanced Certificate of Vocational Education (ACVE, the renamed Advanced GNVQ), and vice versa. However, given the different nature and structure of these courses it is doubtful if this is a realistic option for many students. Many ACVE students may be taking an AS course alongside their vocational course but this happened under the old GNVQ system before Curriculum 2000. So no real progress here!

An integral part of the Curriculum 2000 package was the introduction of Key Skills for all level 3 students, not just those doing vocational courses. Although a laudable aim, the introduction of Key Skills is proving to be a fiasco. Many factors have contributed to this situation, among which are:

- the range of key skills chosen to examine – industry seems to favour the skills of problem-solving, working with others etc. rather than the skills of communication, IT and application of number, which of course are individual and easier to assess

- the skills are difficult to assess within the AS/A2 courses, especially when the time for teaching these courses is squeezed

- not all students were encouraged to take these skills. FE Colleges and Sixth Form Colleges had to offer these courses or else their funding would fall. State schools were under no obligation to offer these courses, and many chose not to. And the private sector schools could, as always, do what they liked, i.e. stick to the old A levels and forget about key skills

- the system for collecting and assessing the portfolio of evidence for awarding the key skills has become a bureaucratic nightmare for teachers/lecturers and students.

While the changes to the academic route have not fulfilled the aspirations of their proponents, the changes to the general vocational route have been disastrous. Apart from the name changes at level 3, from GNVQ Advanced to Vocational A levels to Advanced Certificate of Vocational Education, the alignment of the general vocational route to the academic route serves to question the validity of the general vocational route. This becomes even more acute when most students are using the general vocational route to get into higher education rather than directly into employment. Why go down a route that doesn't have the same esteem as the academic route when the destination appears the same?

One of the distinctive aspects of the GNVQs was the integration of Key Skills into the delivery of the vocational units. With the change to ACVEs this link is now removed. Key skills are not an integrated part of the qualification but are now separate qualifications. Although the teaching of the ACVE may integrate the key skills, such an approach may not appeal to managers who would rather see a single system for delivery of key skills rather than one system for AS/A2 courses and another for ACVE courses.

Another problem that was developing in the old GNVQ system but has become more acute in the ACVE system is the effective breaking of links between the course and the world of work. For a range of reasons, many, if not most, schools and colleges have found it increasingly difficult to sustain work experience as an integral part of the course and have abandoned it. Sometimes this element is replaced with visits or with speakers and in other cases with nothing. Again, an important part of the general vocational route has been lost.

What alternatives can we offer? Firstly the Government must stop seeing this area of education through rosy A level spectacles, and looking over its shoulder at the private sector. The vision needed must be a national system for all; a system that is student-centred, not university-centred. That means a move towards less specialisation post-16, the development of a broader curriculum encompassing vocational and academic options within one framework. Inevitably, such an approach must incorporate the development of a units and credits framework so that students can build up the quali-fication appropriate to them. Such an approach would abolish the end of course examination. It would also make it the responsibility of universities to enroll students, not for colleges and schools to teach to a syllabus based on the requirement of university entry.

Planning

Comprehensive is a word seldom used in relation to education post-16. It seems that the further up the school system you rise the less comprehensive it needs to be. Such an approach is wrong. Compre-hensive education must be the cornerstone on which the system is built. However, in the post-16 sector the structure of comprehensive education needs to be based on geographical areas, not on individual institutions. No individual institution can hope to cover the range of courses and levels that are available to post-16 students. So the provision needs to be on a regional basis. Each area must provide an agreed minimum offer in terms of levels and courses. To be effec-tive, such a system should encompass all the institutions offering education and training to post-16 students in each region. To be effective, each institution offering post-16 education should offer a nationally agreed minimum range of courses and levels so that student travel can be restricted. Although each region must make a minimum offer, this should not exclude it providing other courses specific to the needs of its students.

Within each region there needs to be a planning body which can oversee the provision of the minimum and the extended offer. Such a body must also decide on the allocation of funding for the region. At present much of the post-16 sector, namely Further Education and Sixth Form Colleges, is accountable to itself or to some un-accountable quango. To have effective planning the planning body must represent all the constituencies interested in post-16 education and training, unions, LEA colleges, schools, students, careers staff etc. These representatives must be accountable to their con-stituencies so that the workings of the planning body are open and transparent.

Such a body also needs to ensure that all students have structured tutorial support as well as adequate careers guidance, and that, where necessary, students at any level receive the support they need to achieve their aims. Another important aspect of the planning body is to ensure that bias and discrimination are removed from the system so that the provision is accessible to all students. Such a system would need to be based on cooperation between institutions rather than the competition that still exists today.

Part 2:
Privatisation and the Loss of Democratic Accountability

11

Privatisation and schooling

Richard Hatcher

When Labour came to power the big concern was market relationships among schools driven by parental choice. Now we see that is just part of a much bigger threat. No-one then predicted that today private companies would be running parts, or in the case of Leeds, the whole, of LEAs' services. The existence of schooling as a publicly-run service is under threat from privatisation on a number of fronts, and taking various forms. I shall be focusing here on privatisation in the sense of the private sector providing state education services for profit. I leave aside the spread of other forms of commercialisation, eg advertising and sponsorship in schools.

Why business is moving into schooling

I want to begin with the reasons why business is moving into schooling. From the point of view of business, the key word is globalisation. In the context of heightened international competition, business is driven to seek new potential markets, and the public sector is seen as one of the few major areas still left to colonise. This means a changed role for the state. As the World Bank has said: 'although the state still has a central role in ensuring the provision of basic services – education, health, infrastructure – it is not obvious that the state must be the only provider, or a provider at all.' The global mechanism to open up state education to the private sector is the General Agreement on Trade and Services (GATS), which was part of the agenda at the Seattle round of the World Trade Organisation in 1999.

Why the Government wants business in schooling

The New Labour Government agrees with the World Bank. The principle that the state must guarantee access to certain goods but need not directly provide them is a central tenet of its outlook. Blair says, 'Remember that what matters is outcomes, what matters is what works'. However, this should not be interpreted as a neutral pragmatism towards public or private provision, or as meaning that the private sector is invited in only when the public sector fails – New Labour has an ideological commitment to private participation in public provision. So for example Schools Minister Estelle Morris recently stated that 'Town halls should encourage schools to use private contractors for services traditionally provided by local education authorities'.

Why is the Labour Government so keen to open up education to the private sector? There are two reasons.

- First, business participation is regarded as essential in order to 'modernise' the school system, in terms of innovation, efficiency and accountability.

- Second, the government sees a strong British education industry as a vital new sector in the knowledge economy. That fledgling industry has to be fostered and nourished by the state until it is strong enough to compete with US and other competitors. This provides part of the explanation for such disparate phenomena as the massive state funding for ICT in schools, the attacks on many LEAs for inefficiency, for which the solution is privatisation, not democratisation, and the undermining of all LEAs by the delegation of funding to schools which they can use to purchase services from the private sector (often because the LEAs no longer have the capacity to provide them). The Government is incubating the emerging British 'edubusiness' sector as a viable national and international money-earner, capable of competing in the global market, before it is exposed to the full force of competition from the US edubusiness industry as a result of the free trade in services under a revised GATS.

Privatisation under the Conservative Government

Of course, the private sector has always had an involvement in school education, as a supplier of goods and products. It was under the Thatcher and Major Conservative government that legislation was introduced to enable the private sector to take over the running of some parts of state provision for private profit.

- School inspections were to be carried out by teams who bid for contracts from Ofsted. Many of these teams are private companies, some of which have many teams and carry out hundreds of inspections a year for profit. This has created an industry which is worth over £100 million a year

- The Private Finance Initiative was a new way of funding the construction and running of schools by the private sector.

- The creation of City Technology Colleges as a form of school with direct business sponsorship.

- The privatisation of LEA services:

  - Supply teachers

  - Professional development and consultants

  - Compulsory Competitive Tendering (CCT) for non-teaching services, eg school meals, maintenance.

All of these have continued and flourished under the Labour Government, well before GATS comes into force. Some of the Conservative initiatives have simply been re-branded: CTCs as City Academies, CCT as Best Value, PFI as PPP (Public Private Partnership).

What is the education industry?

I want briefly to consider five main elements:

National government services,
PFI (Profile Finance Initiative),
LEA services,
Schools for profit,
E-learning.

1. Privatisation of national government education services

Perhaps the most obvious example is the administration of performance-related pay (PRP) for teachers. Cambridge Education Associates has been awarded a five-year contract, worth up to £100 million, to help run the PRP system. Head teachers cannot be trusted to assess their own staff, so CEA are deploying 3000 or more assessors to oversee heads' assessments, and to assess the heads' own performance. Another recent example is the contracting-out of professional development for teachers about the National Grid for Learning to a number of private companies.

2. The Private Finance Initiative (PFI)

PFI was launched by the Conservative Government in 1992 as a way of securing private finance for infrastructure projects. It has been continued by New Labour, now renamed the Public Private Partnership (PPP). In education, PPP can finance the construction of new buildings, the renovation of buildings, the provision of equipment and the operation of facilities. The private sector finances construction and is repaid by the state over a period of time (25-35 years) for the use of the building and the facilities. Each PPP project is structured around a specially created company typically combining the construction company, financial institutions and a facilities management company.

To give one example: Colfox school in Dorset is a new comprehensive school, built under a 30 year PPP contract for £15 million by the Jarvis Group, who are responsible for construction plus facilities management: repairs, maintenance, cleaning, catering, utilities, furniture and IT equipment. The largest PPP project is the refurbishment of all 29 secondary schools in Glasgow at a cost of £220 million.

The advantage of PPP for the Government is that it reduces capital spending – or, rather, postpones it to future years. PPP projects also have the advantage of not counting as capital spending under the Maastricht criteria for public sector borrowing. However, it is important to note that PPP is not just about funding capital projects. It entails a redefinition of provision in the public service, as the Government has made clear.

PPP is one of the Government's main instruments for delivering higher quality and more cost effective public services, with the public sector as an enabler and, where appropriate, guardian of the interests of the users and customers of public services. It is not simply about the financing of capital investment in services, but about exploiting the full range of private sector management, commercial and creative skills (press release, Lord Chancellor's department, 8 February 1998).

PPP projects are more expensive than publicly funded projects: it costs local education authorities more to borrow from the private sector than from the Government, and on top of that there are fees for consultants and the profit taken by the PPP companies. It is estimated that PPP projects cost at least 10% more. But they can receive government approval only if they demonstrate 'value for money', so they have to reduce costs by operating schools more efficiently on facilities management contracts which employ fewer staff, on flexible contracts, and which increase income generation through charges for private and community use of school premises.

Like other companies, PPP projects can be the subject of takeovers and mergers, creating, in effect, a market in buying and selling schools. Furthermore, PPP contracts currently do not include the school's core service of teaching, but this distinction between core and non-core services, whereby the private sector controls the infrastructure of buildings and facilities while teachers provide a public service within them, may not be maintained. Future PPP contract bids may include private schools-for-profit companies to provide a total service.

3. Franchising out LEA services

In April 2000 the policy of 'Best Value' came into force. Best Value is the new name for the Conservatives' policy of Compulsory Competitive Tendering, whereby local councils are obliged to consider privatisation as an option for their service provision. A number of LEAs have failed their inspection – almost all in areas of high social disadvantage. The remedy imposed by government in almost all these cases is the handing over of some or all LEA services to private companies. As well as new specialised education-for-profit companies, a number of corporate giants have become government-approved providers, including Group 4, which runs security services including private prisons, and Serco, which runs the UK's air defence warning system against missile attack.

As an example let us take Islington, a London borough which was the first to be privatised. After a critical Ofsted report on the LEA, the Government sent in PriceWaterhouseCoopers, a management accountancy company, to prepare a contract (at a cost of £260,000) for privatising the LEA's services. The contract, for seven years at £11.5 million a year, was awarded to Cambridge Education Associates, who are responsible for personnel and payroll matters, school inspections and school improvement, governor support and special education needs. The contract is subject to tough targets and penalties set by government, and to a cap on profits of £600,000 a year.

4. Running schools

The most controversial aspect of private sector involvement in education has been the proposal that private companies might directly run state schools.

In 1998 Surrey LEA invited companies to bid for the contract to run a 'failing' comprehensive school, King's Manor in Guildford. The contract was won by 3 E's Enterprises Ltd, a private company set up as the commercial arm of Kingshurst City Technology College near Birmingham (about 150 miles away from Guildford). The managing director of 3 E's is the husband of the Kingshurst CTC principal. The contract to run the school entails re-opening it with no guarantee of jobs for existing staff – six were dismissed and are currently engaged in a legal case. Some pupils were excluded too. The implications for local popular influence are interesting: English schools have governing bodies comprising representatives of parents, teachers, the LEA, and the local community (including local business). 3 E's has insisted that it shall nominate 12 of the 21 school governors.

The takeover of King's Manor represents two innovations. One is the franchising of a state school to a private company; the other is the creation by a state school of a commercial subsidiary to operate in the new education market. It is now being held up by the DFEE in the Green paper *Building on Success* as a model to follow.

The most recent government policy initiative facilitating the privatisation of state schools, announced in March 2000, is to set up City Academies (similar to Charter Schools in the US) to replace existing 'failing' schools. They will be directly funded by the government, by-passing LEAs, and given the status of 'independent' – i.e. private – schools, so they will lie outside the legislative framework which governs other state-maintained schools. This includes complete freedom to devise the curriculum. The Government wants them to be run by businesses, churches or voluntary bodies. Sponsors must pay 20% of the capital costs, but ownership of the land and buildings of the existing state school, currently the property of the local council, will be transferred to them. Around 10 are planned to open this year. So far Boots, a national chain of pharmacists, and Reg Vardy, who owns a large chain of car dealers, have expressed an interest in sponsoring City Academies.

5. E-learning – technology and teaching

The transformation of education into a market service is closely tied to the development of information technology, especially the internet. John T Chambers, CEO of Cisco Systems, one of the leading global companies in the field, believes that 'the next big killer application for the Internet is going to be education. Education over the Internet is going to be so big it is going to make e-mail usage look like a rounding error.' In the UK, the Department for Education and Employment (DfEE) is spending £700 million on connecting all 30,000 schools to the Internet by 2002, with a further £230 million to private companies to train teachers to use the new technology. It is a huge partnership between government and the private sector which opens up a vast market for ICT companies. Tony Blair described the initiative at the 1997 Labour Party Conference as 'the biggest public-private partnership in any education system anywhere in the world.'

There are two reasons for the huge investment in ICT in schools.

- ICT is regarded as vital for a profitable labour force in the knowledge economy.

- Massive state spending on ICT in schools and colleges is necessary to stimulate and subsidise the European ICT industry

ICT is expensive not just because of the initial costs but also on account of the continuous need to maintain and update equipment and software, taking perhaps 25% of a school's managed budget. For example, in February 1999 Microsoft launched its Anytime Anywhere Learning initiative (AAL) in the UK. The aim is to provide every pupil with a portable computer. Mark East, Microsoft's Education Group manager, estimates the cost at £8 billion, which has to be 'refreshed every' three years. While the state is funding the initial costs of connecting schools to the Internet, the aim is to seek to transfer some of the running costs directly to parents. Nigel Paine, Chief Executive of the Technology Colleges Trust, suggests 'getting parents to sponsor individual machines'.

It is not just the provision of the hardware and infrastructure which is profitable. The most far-reaching attraction to business of ICT in schools is its potential to transform teaching and learning. ICT requires education content, and this opens up the opportunity to turn teaching and learning into a commodity. Pilot projects are already under way in schools in the UK. For example, Sun Microsystems has formed a partnership with seven other companies and a comprehensive school in Cambridge which is 'working to develop a business model for the local delivery of ICT infrastructure and content', in other words the development for commercial publication of school-produced material. The school has been designated by the EC as a pilot. The school's head of ICT asserts that 'Educational interests come before commercial interests or profit. Our partners are discreet. We have chosen to support them through links to their sites from our school website, and we can provide brochures and documents to those who want them. (...) It's a very business-like arrangement.'

Another example comes from north-east Lincolnshire, where a partnership between the LEA, a private software company and a television company has set up a local cable network which will deliver a package of interactive GCSE materials. This service is already being sold to other schools and LEAs, and marketed as a solution to the shortage of teachers.

The prospects for the private sector

From the business point of view, the prospects are good. Capital Strategies, corporate finance advisers with an interest in education, calculate that the UK education market is currently worth £2.5 billion pa, and estimate it at £5 billion in five years time. For the Labour Government the problem is more complicated: how can it simultaneously satisfy the need for private profitability, meet its own education policy objectives, and minimise professional and public resistance to change? There are real tensions here.

First, education is too important for government to leave to the market. Government has to ensure a school system which meets the general needs of capitalist reproduction of future workers, citizens, families, and the social order, not just the specific interests of the 'education-for-profit' sector. This entails a degree of centralised government control over the school system which may place un-welcome constraints on the operations of private companies.

Second, the level of public funding of the school system may leave little scope for private profit. The problem for the private sector is whether they can make enough profit out of running state schools. The American schools-for-profit company Edison, which runs 108 schools in the US, has investigated the UK market and has decided to withdraw, saying that it will be unable to make enough profit. Ironically, one reason is the low level of state spending on English schools, which is 25% less than for any US school district, and below the threshold which Edison regards as profitable.

Third, the quality of provision by a nascent private sector may not come up to standard. A case in point is the recent abandoning of the privatisation of LEA services in Haringey, London, because the bids from two private companies were rejected as unsatisfactory.

Fourth, much professional and public opinion remains attached to the idea of education as a publicly-provided service.

How privatisation threatens schooling

So what is emerging is not the wholesale privatisation of schooling but the construction of a new settlement between commercial and state interests whose final shape is not yet clear but which includes the large-scale opening up of public provision to private profit. The quasi-privatisation of schooling poses five specific threats.

1) A threat to the funding of education

Business is in the education business to take more money out than they put in. PFI is a good example – the overall cost is more, not less.

2) A threat to local democracy

LEAs and school governing bodies are not exactly models of democracy, but they are still much too interfering for edubusiness's taste.

3) A threat to equality

The introduction of market forces into public services tends to reinforce patterns of inequality. For example, some pupils are more profitable than others, and education-for-profit companies will prefer to cherry-pick their clientele.

4) A threat to the content of education

The more business penetrates the schools the more it will tend to make them conform to business interests eg: advertising on portals, software reflecting business perspectives.

5) A threat to the teaching and learning process

This refers particularly to the role of information technology. Technology is not neutral, it tends to impose its own rhythms. Internet-based teaching lends itself to the individualised acquisition of knowledge and competences, but not to collective dialogue which relates new knowledge to the learner's meanings and experiences. ICT also could represent a threat to teachers' jobs, if it is used as a substitute for teachers.

Responding to the business agenda

The starting point is the recognition that there are two distinct logics at work. One is a logic of education, based on social and individual need, and notions of equity and democracy. The other is a logic of business, whose bottom line is profit. Not everything business wants to do is incompatible with education interests. But the logic of business is incompatible with the logic of education. So the crucial question is, which logic shall predominate? It is a question of power. One way to safeguard the logic of education is to exclude business from any role entailing control over provision. That is both feasible and desirable in the case of the provision of LEA services or the running of schools. But it is not a viable strategy either where the public sector is not in a position to supply an entire service – as is the case with information technology and E-learning – or where business has already taken over service provision – as is the case in some LEAs. There the question is, how can business interests be controlled by education interests? What renewed forms of democracy are needed, at national, local and school levels, to protect public need against private profit?

12

Political Interference: campaigning for a democratic and accountable education service in Leeds

Bob Wood

In early February 2000, Ofsted published a highly critical and damaging report on the Local Education Authority of Leeds City Council. Although the Report acknowledged that Leeds had a higher proportion of successful primary schools than the national average, and that progress was being made under a new Director of Education, it concluded that 'given the sheer volume, depth and range of the authority's failings, this inspection has little confidence in the LEA's capacity to respond fully to the government's agenda within an acceptable timescale.' The Report also complained of a history of 'political interference' in the functioning of the LEA.

In fact, the performance of the LEA in Leeds has been better than that of many other authorities in several respects. A Level results are above the national average. Results at the ages of 7 and 14 are above the national average. More is spent on education in total than central government requires and costs for administration are considerably lower than targets set by the Department for Education and Employment. Moreover, Leeds is in the forefront when it comes to early years provision, and also in the integration of children with special needs into schools.

Following the Ofsted Report, consultants PricewaterhouseCoopers were appointed to consider what should be done next. Their work is reported to have cost Leeds in excess of £200,000. When the Report appeared, it ranked various options in a highly subjective procedure. Total outsourcing of the services provided by the LEA scored the highest number of points, effectively the complete privatisation of the authority. A public-private partnership (a joint venture company) scored almost as highly. The *status quo* was on this occasion at least considered as an option, but appeared well down the list.

In June the Schools Minister, Estelle Morris, finally announced that the preferred option was a Joint Venture Company (JVC), jointly controlled in a 50-50 partnership by Leeds City Council and a private sector partner. The chair of the new company was named in October as Peter Ridsdale, until then known only as the chair of Leeds Sporting plc, the owners of Leeds United.

A shortlist of potential private sector partners was announced in November: Capita (who according to a Radio 4 programme have been far from successful in running housing benefit in Lambeth), WS Atkins (best known as an engineering consultancy), and Serco (who include in their diverse interests the contract for Doncaster Prison).

The choice of partner had been due at the end of January 2001 but was delayed, amid reports that councillors, heads, governors and trade union representatives had all been far less than impressed by the presentations made by all three of the prospective partners. In the interim, the Leader of the Council and all the Leeds MPs (all the parliamentary seats in Leeds are held by Labour) were said to be discreetly lobbying the DfEE for a more acceptable partnership with another local authority, perhaps Birmingham or Lancashire.

After a year of uncertainty, and on the precise anniversary of the original Ofsted Report, the Government finally ditched the Joint Venture Company in favour of an Arms Length Company, fully owned by the City Council, but still with Peter Ridsdale in charge and still employing either Capita or Serco as consultants. As it turned out, Capita were the successful bidders – they already have extensive interests in schools computer information management systems. The final transfer is due in April 2001.

The campaign to prevent any loss of democracy or accountability in the education service, whether it involved an element of privatisation or not, has been led throughout by the Leeds Campaign for the Advancement of State Education (CASE). *The Yorkshire Evening Post* also provided strong support for the campaign, giving extensive coverage to the issues and arguments over the proposals. The Labour Party in the city holds more than three-quarters of the seats on the City Council and has generally been hostile to the removal of the education service from direct control by the Council. But this opposition has often been tempered to some extent by feelings of loyalty to Westminster.

Leeds CASE was launched in June 2000 and public sector trade unions whose members are affected by the proposals have provided the backbone of the campaign. Led by UNISON, the campaign has also had a significant input from both the main teaching unions, the NUT and the NASUWT. Governors, parents and others have also played a role. The campaign has been determined, sustained and per-sistent over a period of many months, with public meetings, lobbies, demonstrations, street stalls, leafleting and many other activities.

The central CASE argument was that education should continue to be controlled, however imperfectly, by the people of Leeds through the mechanism of the ballot box. Any attempt to reduce the accountability of elected representatives for the education service should be resisted. Any suggestion that the private sector is some-how by definition more efficient has been relatively easy to rebut, given the state of the railways.

CASE has also questioned the cost of the exercise. In addition to the costs involved in setting up the new arrangement, the Council will have to maintain a parallel structure to monitor the performance of the new company. Fees or profits earned by the private sector partners will clearly not be available to be spent on education.

Understandably perhaps, the campaign has been less successful in setting what is happening in Leeds in the wider context of a potential global market in education, and the Government's unspoken determination to ensure that UK business is well placed to benefit from this market. It could also be argued that CASE would have benefited from linking up to a greater extent with the opposition inside the Labour Party.

In July, shortly after the Schools Minister had opted for a Joint Venture Company, the Leeds District Labour Party, after a heated debate, resolved to call for the retention of the management of education by the City Council, support for the CASE campaign and a city-wide referendum on the issue. It also called for the Labour Group on the council to publicly oppose the Government's proposals. Although this had little apparent effect, it did indicate the strength of opinion within the party.

When an adjournment debate on the issue took place in the House of Commons in July 2000, all the Leeds MPs expressed doubts about the way in which the DfEE was dealing with Leeds LEA, albeit with varying degrees of fervour. Following the marginal concession that the JVC would be replaced by an arms length company, the MP for Leeds East, George Mudie, a former leader of the Council, complained that a council which had seen off Margaret Thatcher should have no difficulty with Estelle Morris. The Council's preference for a partnership with another local authority was roundly ignored, but their opposition and the opposition within the party have never been translated into votes in the council chamber. At the time of writing, the campaign continues. The Lord Mayor has offered to lead a delegation to Blunkett 'if the people of Leeds want me to', and letters are appearing nightly in the evening press encouraging him to do so.

In its report in February 2000, Ofsted wrote of the 'Government's agenda' and the need for the LEA to respond to it. Unfortunately, the Government's agenda appears to have more to do with the needs of British business than with public education and the defence of the comprehensive ideal. Leeds may have been chosen for this experiment because it is the second largest LEA. Although its performance is better than that of Sheffield or Hull, it does not have a cabinet minister to embarrass.

The last word should perhaps go to the *Yorkshire Evening Post* (editorial comment, 14 June 2000): 'This snub to Leeds is nothing less than an outrageous affront to democracy which divorces us all from the right to take a part in our children's education. And if this untested experiment fails they will be the ones to pay the price.'

13

The Market in Education

John Yandell

I work at a secondary school in Hackney, East London. At the start of this year, there was a Year 7 class in the school which had no regular, permanent teachers for English, maths, science, humanities, French, music, art, physical education or drama. They had a form tutor and a technology teacher – and that was it. In the vast majority of their timetabled lessons, they could look forward to being supervised by a succession of supply teachers. The situation that this class found itself in was atypical, even for my school. But it marks one end of a continuum. Teachers are in such short supply, particularly in London and in the Home Counties, that it can be difficult to address larger questions of curriculum and assessment as anything other than matters of mere theoretical interest. For the children in 7G, questions around the content of humanities, for example, as well as issues of pedagogy or assessment, are likely to be less pressing than questions about the identity (or existence, even) of their humanities teacher next week, next month, next term.

And yet if one asks what lies behind the current shortage, it is hard to go very far towards providing an explanation for the predicament in which 7G find themselves before one turns to matters of curriculum and assessment. Of course the teacher shortage is a product of economic conditions – the cost of living in South East England, house prices, teachers' wages. Of course the shortage has been exacerbated by the long-term underfunding of education and its consequences for the everyday lives of teachers and pupils in state schools: the unspeakable physical conditions in which many of us are expected to work and to learn. But it is also hard to avoid the fact of widespread teacher demoralisation and disaffection – or the suspicion that much of this bad feeling stems from the imposition from above of curriculum content and organisation, and even more so from the creation of a monstrous regime of testing.

In the week before this Conference, I had to break up a fight between two Year 10 students at my school. (They were not in my class; their English lesson was being covered by a supply teacher.) I became aware of a commotion on the corridor. When I went to see what was going on, I found Gideon, brandishing a chair. It became clear that he wanted to inflict serious physical injuries on another student, Aaron. I managed to relieve Gideon of his chair. He then rampaged around the corridor, entering classroom after classroom in search of other chairs. I followed him, seeking to dissuade him and relieving him of each chair he selected. Gideon then abandoned his pursuit of an appropriate chair and started to pick up the tables instead. After hurling a couple of these as far as he could, he tried to take one out into the corridor, again in pursuit of Aaron. Eventually, having been shepherded away from other students, Gideon calmed down. He and Aaron told me what the fight had been about.

This was, as I hope is clear, a serious incident. For a few minutes, Gideon had been beside himself with rage, intent on damaging another student. Both students agreed that the conflict had started when Gideon had said that Aaron was 'dumb'. 'You're calling me 'dumb'?' Aaron had replied. 'Right. I got level 5s in my SATs. What did you get? Oh, Gideon. Level 2s, innit?' And so it all began.

It is possible that the two students would have found something else to argue about if the SATs had not existed – that a fight might have been triggered by a multitude of other insults. That, though, is hardly the point. The fact is that Gideon had been publicly humiliated because of a label that had been attached to him by the tests that have come to occupy so prominent a place in the education landscape. Both students – and all the others in their vicinity – were (and are) victims of a system which sets student against student, teacher against teacher, school against school. The fight had its origins not in the tables which Gideon overturned but in the tests which help him to see Aaron as a competitor, an enemy, and in the league tables which label their school as a failure.

The last Tory Government was responsible for the creation of a kind of market in education, but this market has been perpetuated by the present Government. As Michael Prowse wrote recently in the *Financial Times* (27 January 2001):

> *The Blair Government, like its Tory predecessors, behaves as though the mythical 'economic men' of microeconomic text-books describe real human beings. It behaves as though people are always self-regarding and can be motivated only by carrots and sticks.*
>
> *This is why it relies so heavily on league tables and hundreds of absurd numerical targets. It thinks the only way you can get a doctor or a teacher (or indeed anyone) to perform well is to reward or punish them personally according to their success in meeting some externally set targets.*
>
> *This is wrong, wrong, wrong. ...*
>
> *The public sector should be recognised for what it is: a co-operative venture to promote the common good that is based on ethical principles. The goal should be to achieve uniformly high standards (while recognising the inevitability of some varia-tions) by predominantly rational rather than market means.*

It is a striking feature of this Government's intervention in education that it manages to accentuate divisions even when it seems to be attempting to address structural inequality. The Excellence in Cities initiative was meant to provide more resources where they were most needed, to target areas of disadvantage. What happens in practice? It becomes a mechanism to pacify a middle class minority, by identifying and isolating the so-called 'gifted and talented'. Mr Blair helps those who have already had a generous helping. Children whose experience of the education system has already been largely positive are encouraged to achieve more – are indeed enabled to achieve more – by being told how much more able they are than their peers. It is hard to see how such assessments help Gideon or the thousands of others who have already been failed by the system, tested and found wanting.

There are, nevertheless, aspects of the Government's education programme that have worked against the atomisation of the market. In both the content of the curriculum and in the area of pedagogy, Blair and his aides have been reluctant to leave it up to market forces. From primary schools, where the Literacy and Numeracy Hours now occupy so much of teachers' and pupils' time, to higher education, where the content of initial teacher education courses is specified in ever-increasing detail by government, the message is clear: there is one true path to enlightenment, and Michael Barber knows the way. The approach to teaching and learning is a technicist one. Big questions are generally best avoided. Spend time in the naming of parts, not in making connections between them. Children are taught to spot adjectives, rather than to use language to make sense of the world around them. They read 'literacy texts' – not books.

There are contradictions here that will take time to be worked out. Already there are signs that pupils are not prepared to accept the passive, unquestioning role in which such models of teaching and learning cast them. Disaffection is a product of the current system. There are also opportunities for us to make criticisms of the present regime and to pose alternatives. Within the past decade, the SATs boycott provided an example of the kind of united campaign, involving parents, governors, school students as well as teachers, in which it is possible to mount a sustained critique of curriculum and assessment. More recently, there have been similarly broad-based local campaigns – such as the successful fight against privatisation fought at Pimlico School, Westminster, or the protests against the imposition of an Education Action Zone in Hackney – which have opened up the space for debate about all aspects of education – including curriculum and assessment. This is the way we need to go.

Part 3:
Conclusion

14

Responding to the themes of the collection

Ken Jones

E ssentially four themes have been raised in this book. The first is our concern about New Labour's education programme, a wide-ranging programme that touches all areas of the lives of those who work or study, or who are parents: piecemeal responses will not adequately take the measure of the programme.

Second is that New Labour's programme is in many respects international. That is to say, it derives its arguments and its motivations not just from the thoughts of Tony Blair and David Blunkett but from those various inter-governmental and international organisations and think-tanks which have been promoting, at least since the middle 1980s, a new agenda for education in the advanced capitalist countries. That agenda is what is now being pursued in Britain. It isn't a local peculiarity, it's something that's being experienced in many parts of the world, not least in continental Europe. People who are concerned about the same issues as we are can be found also in Italy, France, Germany. And the links that it's possible to make with these experiences, and those other resistances, are very important for our understanding and capacity to act. Far more than ever before, what's happening to us in the form of privatisation and the emergence of business agendas is happening, and almost at the same pace, in neighbouring countries, as a globalised project for reshaping education meets with local circumstances in which, in the past, education and its purposes have been conceived in quite other ways. These conflicts between the globalised agenda and more local and resistant forms are present in many places in Europe, and it's important that we connect ourselves with them. That's my second point.

The third issue is that although there are opportunities for some progressive change, in most respects New Labour's policies are wrong. They are having unacceptable effects on the system, at several levels, not least at the level of equality. But in addition to that, this programme – which has been so carefully devised and which will accelerate after the next election – is also one that is troubled by the possibility of opposition. Opposition both silent and more explicit and organised. For instance, when a senior government policy advisor was interviewed, towards the beginning of Labour's period in office, by some of my colleagues, they asked him what he thought the main problem was for the implementation of the government's educational programme. His answer was instant, brief and eloquent: teachers. Not teachers' pay, nor conditions. Just – teachers. An education system, no matter how well designed at the top level, unfortunately has this flaw of needing to depend at local level on the interaction of groups of people who aren't finally controllable – namely teachers, students, and all those others who are interested parties in the school. New Labour's programme can be seen from one angle as an attempt to control these interactions. It's a very determined attempt, it's a very detailed attempt, but in its hostility to difference, to the interests of other actors, and to the knowledge and experiences which can't be accounted for in centralised planning, it has the flaw of every grand design.

An explicit indication of the way government puzzles over this problem may be seen in the contributions of Michael Barber, Head of the Standards and Effectiveness Unit. Last year, with Vicki Phillips, he addressed a conference on Education Action Zones and came up with an interesting formula which was – I think – originally developed in the seventeenth century by Blaise Pascal, though it may have been filtered through management theory since. Pascal had a theory about prayer, and indeed about belief generally. Essentially, he argued, you learn to pray by first going down on your knees. Only thus will you create the conditions for belief, and be able to address God accordingly. Barber and Phillips, taking up the analogy, pursue the question 'how can minds be won in education, how can consent be won for Labour's education programme?' And the answer they came up with is completely specific: you don't try to change minds through argument, consultation, debate, dialogue. You change them first of all through changing people's behaviour, through the element of compulsion. Down on your knees first, then you can worship at the appropriate shrine. Here is the argument verbatim:

> There is a popular misconception about the process of change. It is often assumed that the key to successful change is 'to win hearts and minds'. If this is the starting point then the first steps in the process of change are likely to be consultation and public relations campaigns. ... The popular conception is wrong. Winning hearts and minds is not the best first step in any process of urgent change. Beliefs do not necessarily shape behaviour. More usually it's the other way round – behaviours shape beliefs. Only when people have experienced a change do they revise their beliefs accordingly ... Sometimes it is necessary to mandate the change, implement it well, consciously challenge the prevailing culture, and then have the courage to sustain it until beliefs shift ... The driving force at this critical juncture is leadership.

Explicit here is a theory of change which runs deep in the programme we're discussing today. It attempts to create a system in which all parties (but one) have, as it were, forgotten the habit of argument; in which what is dictated centrally dominates the agenda to a striking extent. That, I think, is a planner's dream, far more extensive and intrusive than the government economic projects and national plans which Labour in its present guise would deride the 1960s for entertaining. And like any dream, it contains its element of fantasy, in this case a fantasy of control extending across a wider front than at any other period of British educational history.

The vigour and determination of this programme creates serious problems for many of us. But it is also a problem for government itself; it is afflicted by an irresolvable dilemma. Slacken off, and you allow oppositional voices and practices to appear once again. Maintain strict control, and you fuel a great resentment. We'll see this dilemma working itself out during Labour's second term. But one thing seems clear even now: it's not possible to make an educational system march entirely in step with the dictates of government, however powerfully you apply various behavioural stimuli. And that would be my third point, which applies, I would say, almost as much to parents and students as it does to teachers. Conflicts over the system's fundamental 'regime' – the conceptions of authority and legitimacy which underlie it – will continue to be endemic in schooling's medium term future. Who has the right to participate in discussions about education's meaning, value, purpose and procedures will remain a permanent, and troubling, issue for New Labour.

The last issue is really a question. What possibilities are there within this system to address questions of change, which are necessarily questions of opposition? What strikes me here is that we've heard at this Conference about many different aspects and consequences of New Labour's programme, and that within these comments and critiques are hints about what might be involved in a different system of education, informed by meanings and values very different from those which dominate our present. Unless we can convey a sense of these values, the various campaigns in which we're involved won't create the impact they could have. We need, in other words, to think about joined-up opposition as much as Tony Blair talks about joined-up government. That sort of opposition isn't just a question of sector linking to sector. It's also about linking questions of immediate political moment – streaming, selection, privatisation or whatever – to questions of meaning and value, as they affect our vision of education's purposes.

Issues of this sort seem to me to be fundamental to the reconstruction of a movement for educational change, and their importance is underlined by recent events in Llanwern and the other steel towns. 'In their hearts,' we were told by a BBC correspondent, who numbers clairvoyance among his journalistic gifts, 'these men know there is no alternative to closure'. I doubt this. But I do not doubt that the movement against closure can learn much from the 1930s and the decimations and defeats suffered by those who worked in industrial areas then. The opposition people in the 1930s were capable of organising, whether about welfare and security, or about jobs, was not immediately successful. But it was capable of doing what the BBC correspondent is so certain that the steelworkers of today cannot do: it was capable of making a case, a popular case, against the effects of free-market, gold standard economics that was so strong that less than a generation later it could provide the basis of support for the Welfare State, for the nationalisation of basic industries and those other achievements which for four decades kept the free marketeers at bay. Not perfect achievements, but the result of an earlier determination not to follow the laws of the market which were laid down as fixed and unalterable wisdom.

Something similar, I think, is our obligation now. We can't operate on the basis of immediate or certain victory. We can't turn the clock back to an earlier period. We have to face this present situation, with all its limitations. But what we should never forget is that what is at stake in all the arguments is not only the fate of single, particular, discrete, desirable or undesirable reforms. It is much more than that. We are facing a restructuring of education that more than ever subjects local policy to the supposed imperatives of market-driven globalisation. What need to be proclaimed, conversely, in the moment of all our activities are the issues of value, of equity, of democracy which we intuitively feel supply the motivation for what we do, but which to our cost we are not always good at articulating.

We can look for international support and inspiration in many areas. To France, where popular protest forced the resignation of a neo-liberal Education Minister. To Italy, where hundreds of thousands of teachers have marched against plans for performance pay. What we can't afford to do is to live and work now in a dispersed way that accepts the very limited agendas that are being forced upon us in our various sectors.

---

*   Michael Barber and Vicki Phillips, 'How to Unleash Irreversible Change: Lessons for the Future of System-Wide School Reform'. Paper to EAZ Conference March 2000.

Part 4:
Additional Essays

15

Blair on Education*

Brian Simon

I approached writing this article with a feeling of disgust. It was motivated by a full front-page report in the *Guardian* early in September (9 September 2000) headlined 'Blair Plans Schools Revolution'. This was just before the fuel crisis and other discontents led to a substantial drop in Labour's poll support: but *after* a rise for Labour in the polls. The party, Mr Blair is reported as saying, had never had more confidence in its values and ideas.

But what light did Blair's speech on education throw on these 'values and ideas? Reported as addressing 'a group of modernising Labour activists in Bedfordshire' (known, apparently, as 'Progress'), Blair used this opportunity to level an all-out, indeed vicious, attack on comprehensive education. This, indeed, is the essence of his speech and must have been designed deliberately to shock. The *Guardian*'s chief political correspondent, Patrick Wintour, stressed that Blair showed his determination 'to break up the failing model of comprehensive schools in England and Wales', demanding greater help for the most gifted pupils in the state sector'. The term 'failing model' applies here presumably to comprehensive schools in general throughout both countries (England and Wales) – or this is how it reads.

Not content with this level of abuse, Blair went on to make further wild, generalised charges. Too often, he said, 'comprehensives adopted a one-size-fits-all mentality – no setting, uniform provision

* This chapter first appeared in *Forum*, Volume 42, Number 3, Autumn 2000

for all, hostility to the notion of specialisation and centres of excellence within areas of the curriculum'. Repeating the right-wing criticisms of the past, Blair rammed this point home. Comprehensives should 'cease meaning the same for all'. The 'Old Left' had played into the hands of the Right by failing to recognise that 'children do have different abilities and aptitudes' and that schools should provide for these. Mounting his clearest indictment yet of the comprehensive principles of the 1960s and 1970s the *Guardian* report goes on. Blair came to the pith of his message:

> *We expect every secondary school to do its best for high ability pupils through first rate teaching and facilitates, rigorous setting and personalised provision. Comprehensives should be as dedicated as any private school or old grammar school to high achievement for the most able.*

Tony Blair is leader of the Labour Party and prime minister. But this sort of assessment takes us right back to the abuse comprehensive education suffered under Margaret Thatcher and John Major – the blanket charge of uniformity, that schools are all the same, talent unrecognised, that generally the whole exercise has been a failure. Caroline Benn and Clyde Chitty's massive study *Thirty Years On* gave the lie to these assertions or, better, myths promulgated by those fundamentally opposed to the whole project of comprehensive secondary education.

Further, these notions are historically uninformed, indeed ignorant. Comprehensive education swept the country because the mass of popular opinion was no longer prepared to tolerate the divisive system inherited from the past. They wanted a changeover to the single secondary school capable of opening up opportunities for all. This they achieved (if partially). The schools so brought into being had to find their own way in the new circumstances. Thanks especially to the devoted work of the teachers, they did this successfully. In spite of the trauma of reorganisation, examination results, in O level and CSE and later in GCSE and at A level, improved steadily year by year. This is a brilliant success story and should be celebrated as such, and not only by Labour as very many others were closely involved.

The present Labour government could have built on this: many, including this author, expected them to complete the comprehensive revolution, to eradicate weaknesses, and deliberately to take things further in a planned and rational manner. But what happened? Comprehensive schools never received a word of support from either Blunkett or Blair. The latter did not hesitate to describe our system as 'rotten' before an international audience. Every effort was made to distance the leadership from the comprehensive reform. Insurmountable barriers were erected against local populations wishing to finalise reorganisation. Trusting people were deliberately misled by ministers (e.g. 'read my lips' from Blunkett). And now the prime minister himself launches a deliberate, populist assault on all that has been achieved. It is almost unbelievable.

Blair's concept of a successful comprehensive school appears to be a cross between Eton, Winchester and the Manchester Grammar School. But this, of course, is ludicrous. 'Personalised' education is certainly desirable (and provided), but to do this effectively means doubling the staff. 'Private schools' with their endowments, may be able to afford this, but not state schools – at least not under the present dispensation. To pretend, or argue otherwise, is pure hypocrisy.

Looking back, one has to admit that the Labour Party has always had an ambiguous relationship to comprehensive education. I have a particular interest in all this since, as assistant secretary to the newly constituted Education Advisory Committee in 1938/39, I was present at two or three intensive discussions culminating in the decision to recommend a transition to comprehensive (then 'multi-lateral') schools, as soon as the opportunity was there. This committee included Chuter Ede, R.H. Tawney, Lionel Elvin and several Labour MPs (e.g. Cove), and the decision was accepted by the executive committee (it was my job to keep the minutes of these meetings and I still have them). However when opportunity did present itself through the post-war Attlee government, Ellen Wilkinson, the appointed minister, instead followed the Board of Education's line, energetically establishing the tripartite (selective) system of secondary education. Attitudes changed in the 1950s and 1960s with the growing popular revolt against the 11+ and now at last the party strongly reiterated its support for comprehensive schools while Tory governments continued to reinforce selection.

The 1964 election, reinstating a Labour Government after thirteen years, provided another opportunity. But now again the party eschewed legislation – Circular 10/65 merely 'requested' local authorities to present plans for the transition. The bulk did so, but not all. There were later missed opportunities also. The net outcome has been that we do not yet have an effective and cohesive system of comprehensive secondary education. And just now, when the opportunity is certainly there again, the Labour leadership finds it necessary to launch a vicious attack on the whole project as at present conceived. That, at least, is how Blair's speech reads, even if it does not propose the actual demolition of the system – rather its 'modernisation' according to criteria established by the government.

Thus Blair lauds the so-called Excellence in Cities project designed, we are told, 'to help gifted children in urban schools', with which more than 1000 'specialist' schools are to be involved. Also (big deal) there are to be six 'specialist city academies' based on the failed model of the Tory city technology colleges.

How was Blair's 'Progress' speech received? Two days after its delivery the *Guardian* published a sample of more or less furious letters from comprehensive supporters. One had put his five children successfully through comprehensive schools and protested strongly at the new divisions within such schools presaged by Blair, who 'is going to have many successful, comprehensively educated, parents opposing him'. 'They don't want their kids consigned to the dustbin'. Another, governor of 'an excellent comprehensive school and Labour party member' was 'doubly mortified' by Blair's comment, angrily rebutting his 'one size for all' claim. Other letters denied the charge of 'failure' which, it was suggested, was better directed at aspects of the government's policy. Not a single letter supported Blair.

The only comment the *Guardian* printed with its initial report of Blair's speech was that of John Dunford, general secretary of the Secondary Heads Association, which unites most comprehensive school heads in the country. He also 'reacted angrily' to Blair's assessment of comprehensive schools. 'I think it is scandalous that the prime minister should be caricaturing the state educational system with a description which is not based on reality'. 'Personal provision' as demanded by the prime minister, 'requires... doubling the amount of money that state schools receive'.

The most consistent publicist promoting comprehensive education within the Labour party is Roy Hattersley, who has been closely involved with the campaign for many years. At the recent Labour Conference in late September he expounded his views following Blair's intervention. 'Comprehensive education', he is reported as saying, has proved a remarkable success. Yet comprehensive schools 'are continually denigrated by the prime minister – often in language which suggests that he has no idea how selective schools are organised and run' (*Guardian*, 26 September 2000). During the eighteen years of Tory government, he goes on, 'we could console ourselves that once Labour was elected things would get better. But the hard truth is that as far as comprehensive education is concerned they have got worse. Despite David Blunkett's promise – 'no selection by examination or interview' – there is more selection now than there was on the day he became secretary of state for education. In another article at this time (*Guardian* 25 September 2000) Hattersley claimed that 'Labour has done more to damage comprehensive education, diminish civil liberties and stigmatise asylum seekers than John Major's Conservatives ever did'. Over the last three years 'the political spectrum has moved to the Right'. Hattersley is not given to wild statements. These are his considered views.

What is to be done? Opposition to Blair's policies on secondary education has been mounting. In April this year Martin Johnson, incoming President of the NAS/UWT, who has taught in some of London's most challenging schools and is author of an acclaimed book *Failing Schools, Failing City,* launched what the *Guardian* called 'a blistering attack' on Tony Blair, claiming that he was systematically 'dismantling the comprehensive schools system by building on 'elitist education policies introduced by the Tories' (*Guardian*, 25 April 2000). The 'so-called specialist and beacon schools' (Blair's main 'modernising' ploy), funded more generously than others, were creating a new hierarchical structure – indeed 'threatened to undermine the whole comprehensive secondary school structure and a system', he concluded, 'now being dismantled'. The gap between good and poor state schools 'was being widened under Labour', a point tellingly made by Nick Davies in his brilliant series of *Guardian* articles earlier in the year. Johnson's union opposed the expansion of a structure of differentiated secondary schools 'as inequitable and damaging to teachers and pupils alike'. To this a DfEE spokesman weakly replied 'we want all schools to be centres of excellence'. That is why 'we give beacon schools and specialist schools extra help so they can spread their expertise to other local schools' (*ibid.*). But who has determined on this policy? What consultations have there been? After all, it is taxpayers' money which is at stake.

The whole situation is profoundly unsatisfactory. But it appears that some people's patience is becoming exhausted. Supporters of the Labour government are naturally muted, or inhibited in their criticism – who wants to rock the boat? Nevertheless, profound dissatisfaction with the Labour leadership's policies on secondary education erupted at the annual conference of the Socialist Education Association in the summer (2000). A vigorous discussion on comprehensive education was the first item on the agenda, the resolution calling on the government to end selection at 11 and (significantly) opposing the expansion of specialist schools. The SEA is the direct successor of the National Association of Labour Teachers which pioneered the campaign for comprehensive education in the 1920s. Its membership includes many MPs and it is in a good position to influence policy. At its summer conference this year the Association drafted a fine education manifesto for the next election, strongly supportive of comprehensive education, announced a fringe meeting at the Labour party conference in September under the heading 'Building on the Success of Comprehensive Education' with Roy Hattersley as the main speaker, and an all-day conference on comprehensive education to be held in early February 2001. A set of excellent speeches by delegates to the SEA conference was reprinted in their journal Education Politics which also includes all conference resolutions.

All this took place before the delivery of Blair's provocative speech to the Bedfordshire 'Progress' group in early September. The petrol crisis, with its threat to the government's authority, swamped reaction to these comments, but it is no doubt they will have a long-term effect. They have alerted comprehensive enthusiasts (and they *are* many) to the real, till now, muted, attitude of some of the leadership, including, and very specifically, the prime minister. These need to be convinced that an 'inclusionary' society *requires* the single secondary school as *the key* condition for its achievement, and that 'rigorous setting' and other forms of differentiation within the schools are not the best way of achieving the unified school which values all equally. Manchester Grammar School and Winchester cannot realistically be accepted as models for *comprehensive* schools. The central objective of comprehensive education was to open new opportunities for all, not just the few – and so generally to raise the standards of all. Concentration specifically on 'the most able', rigid differentiation within comprehensive schools: measures such as these will not reinforce this project – rather the opposite.

The long struggle for comprehensive secondary education, therefore, now enters a new phase. The enemy (if that is the right word) is not the traditional, or the wild, Tory Right. It is the Labour leadership itself, which has the power to make desirable changes but appears to be acting in the opposite direction, actually giving new currency to, and repeating, the arguments of the discredited Tory Right. Clearly it would be best to win over the leadership to a fuller understanding of what the comprehensive reform is all about. Failing that, an all-out struggle may well be needed to win, once more, the political clout necessary to make the change. In the course of this it will be vital to clarify the constitutional position: *who* makes policy? And how? Major initiatives now 'emerge' (e.g. specialist schools) which could transform the structure of the system as a whole. Such an outcome of the years of struggle that have taken place on this issue is totally unacceptable.

16
Specialisation with tiers?
Tony Edwards and Patrick Eavis

The Labour Government's intention that almost every other comprehensive in England should be a specialist school by 2006 develops a main theme from its first (1997) Education White Paper. It was claimed then that while a commitment to common secondary schooling was understandable in the flush of enthusiasm for comprehensive reform, the consequent 'tendency to uniformity' brought with it a damaging mediocrity. Modernising the 'comprehensive principle' now required more schools to develop 'their own distinctive identity and purpose'. This was a proper response to the diversity of children's interests and abilities. The resulting stimulus to innovation in those schools would also contribute to a general raising of educational standards. Inheriting around 200 specialist schools from the Conservatives, the incoming Government accordingly 'relaunched' and expanded the programme. By September 2000 there were 536 such schools, more than the 450 which David Blunkett initially hoped for by the end of the new Parliament. That the target is now 1500 by the year 2006 is a notable example of taking something which the Conservatives had done, and doing it bigger and better.

Yet the old order being reformed was caricatured in Tony Blair's attack on 'one size fits all' comprehensives. Schools vary considerably in what they do and how they do it, despite successive governments' efforts at prescription. Indeed, it is not long since they were less often blamed for uniformity than for experimenting too much with children's education, the first version of the National Curriculum being designed to establish a wide range of 'knowledge, skills and understanding' to which all children were entitled wherever they lived and went to school. But that extensive version has since been sufficiently reduced to leave schools a great deal of scope for innovation and student choice, even without the inducements of specialist status. What Ministers have still not explained is *why* promoting curriculum diversity *between* schools is necessary to modernise the system when excessive and premature specialisation has been a long-standing criticism of English secondary education, and when the demands of a modern economy are usually described in terms of general skills and adaptability.

We should not exaggerate how much specialisation the Government is promoting. One subject area is enriched (technology, languages, arts, or sports) within what should remain a 'broad and balanced' curriculum, and not more than 10% of the intake can be selected on grounds of aptitude for it. It is true that quantified performance targets have to be met in that specialism, which can tempt schools to give it more lesson time or make it compulsory longer than would otherwise be the case. Other subjects may then be crowded out, or normal national curriculum requirements 'disapplied' to allow students to pursue their school's declared strength.

It is not apparent, however, that specialist schools are doing distinctively well in that specialism, as might reasonably be expected. Indeed, a DfEE-commissioned survey of all those established by September 1997 reported that while almost half the headteachers claimed that the specialist area had already been or had become their school's strongest, more than half located its main curriculum strength elsewhere.[1] Certainly the additional resources which specialist status brings may well benefit other parts of the curriculum. Schools are well practised in using apparently earmarked funding for other or wider educational purposes. When Dame Tamsyn Imison defended the programme as head of a technology college (Hampstead School), she emphasized that the extra money had not been used to unbalance the curriculum, but rather to support with better resourced ICT a general shift towards more independent learning.[2] So why is such limited and variable specialisation assumed by the Labour Government to be self-evidently a good thing? And why do we worry about the consequences of the policy?

John Major's Government presented specialist schools as a logical step towards a market system in which previously suppressed consumer demand for variety would be released, and consumer choice extended well beyond better and worse forms of the same model. Given its habit of citing the private sector as exemplifying all the virtues of customer control, the absence of curriculum diversity in most of it would have been inconvenient and so was ignored. The Labour Government's commitment to specialist schools has sometimes been interpreted as a strategy for retaining or even attracting back to the state system the kinds of middle-class families whose 'mass decampment' into private schooling has been described (and exaggerated) in a book co-authored by one of Mr Blair's principal education policy advisers.[3] But there is no evidence of consumer demand for significant departures from the traditional academic curriculum. What education-conscious parents are likely to seek, in both public and private sectors, is a school which offers very good results in that curriculum and therefore good prospects of entry to the most desirable universities and employment. In short, they want a school which differs only in being 'better'. And in practice, the Labour Government's principal argument in favour of specialist schools has been that they are indeed better.

Ministers assumed their superiority before there was relevant evidence for it. They can now cite David Jesson's analysis of all 1997-99 GCSE results, which showed specialist schools overall to have done better, to have produced greater improvements, and to be over-represented both among England's 'best' and its 'most improving' comprehensive schools. In 1999 for example, the proportion of their students achieving five or more A*-C passes, was 53 % compared with 42% in non-specialist comprehensives. For supporters of the 'comprehensive principle', his findings gain weight because his analysis of examination statistics also led him to reject the relative advantage still attributed to grammar schools, and to local authorities retaining considerable numbers of them. His own conclusion is that specialist comprehensive schools offer the best chance of resisting a return to selection, and of avoiding a further decline in public support for comprehensive schooling.[4]

The value-added analysis which showed their superiority did not include any measure of social background. In 1997, specialist schools had significantly fewer pupils eligible for free school meals (the usual indicator of social disadvantage) than the average for English maintained secondary schools. Those admitted to the programme since 1997 have been less associated with social advantage. But the overall lead in school performance conceals a range of results sufficiently wide to question the beneficial effects of specialisation as such. The year 2000 GCSE results show that 38% of specialist comprehensive schools had 60% or more of their students getting five or more A*-C passes, while 17% of those schools had fewer than 40% reaching that threshold. The equivalent figures for schools established since 1997 are 26% and 29%. Either specialisation had not yet had time to bring its benefits or, as we discuss later in this chapter, the later additions to the programme are less advantaged by the social composition of their intakes.

If demonstrating superior performance is difficult, explaining what survives scrutiny is obviously harder still. Avoiding affirming their predecessors' faith in the stimulating effects of competing with other schools by finding a distinctive market niche, Labour Ministers have usually found the causes in the clearer sense of collective purpose which applying and winning specialist status creates, in the development planning and target setting which are conditions for achieving and retaining it, and in the stimulus to improved learning and teaching which is diffused from the specialism to other parts of the curriculum. What are discounted as explaining (or explaining away) the schools' performance are their enhanced resources and the scope for partial selection. Most of the schools included in the survey cited earlier certainly claimed that they had been challenged to focus more sharply on the kind of school they wanted to be, with consequent improvements in teacher and student motivation. That research did not compare those characteristics, nor the extent of innovations in learning, with non-specialist schools. It did report, however, that the opportunity to gain extra resources was the most frequently mentioned reason for applying for specialist status.. The inducements are capital funding of £100,000 provided that private sponsorship worth £50,000 has been secured, and an addition to the recurrent budget (currently £123 per pupil) for each of the initial three years, with the possibility of renewal. The schools surveyed had spent an average £200,000 on capital projects, and an average £108,000 additional recurrent funding on extra full-time teachers and technicians.

These tangible benefits are described by Jesson as 'fairly marginal' because they are unlikely to amount to more than 5% of a school's total budget. His phrase is misleading. Even without the new capital funding, the extra recurrent money gives schools scope for supporting projects beyond their normal resources. It may be 'only' £100,000 or so, but it is 'money not already committed to sustaining ongoing expenditure'. It is therefore money which can be spent on new developments without having to make corresponding reductions elsewhere. In a non-specialist Northumberland high school for example, over-full and with a very large sixth form, only one year during 1991-7 produced a working surplus on a budget of well over £2 million. That sum of £60,000 was promptly spent on re-forming and re-equipping a Resources Centre. This is a priority likely to be supported by specialist schools, but with a good deal more money to do so. This does not seem to us to be a 'fairly marginal' advantage. Nor is it easily reconciled with the Education Secretary repeated promises of 'fair funding'.

The initial requirement of £100,000 of private funding so obviously favoured schools in more affluent areas or with a reputation attractive to local business that the Labour Government reduced it to £50,000 while continuing to emphasize, perhaps even more strongly, close links with sponsors. The extra money from public and private sources, significant in itself, is likely to make it easier to get other grants from other sources on the grounds that they would be building on success or enhancing projects already under way. As is true generally of schools' increasing reliance on sponsorship and parental contributions, private funding 'makes the rich get richer'. It is true that in contrast to its predecessor, which positively encouraged schools to follow market logic by using any advantage to outpace their competitors, the Labour Government has insisted that the special expertise and resources of specialist schools are shared with the local 'family of schools' and the local community. But although the survey cited earlier reported a good deal of sharing with primary schools, there appeared to have been much less sharing with other comprehensive schools. Even if help is offered, it may not be easy to accept it from an 'equal' better resourced and perhaps able to fill its places, especially in areas where schools compete fiercely for applicants.

These remain, in our view, strong reasons for fearing that non-specialist schools may be left behind. Variety without hierarchy was the declared objective of the Conservatives' 1992 White Paper *Diversity and Choice*, even though market logic surely requires winners and losers. While the Labour Government is certainly not intending to reinforce or extend tiers of secondary schooling, its encouragement of diversity – more religious schools, more specialist schools, beacon schools and city academies – carries that risk in a country (England) which has traditionally found it peculiarly difficult to regard different kinds of school as both different and equal. In this context, specialist comprehensive schools have advantages which go well beyond their enhanced resources.

The most obvious of these is usually discounted. School-level performance, although not of course the success or failure of individual students, is highly predictable from the social and academic composition of the intake. Does the right of specialist schools to select part of their intake by aptitude give them more than their share of pupils from whom good results are rather easier to obtain? In practice, and apart from the twenty grammar schools (and fifteen 'modern' schools) on the current list, very few have taken up the option. If the Conservatives had won in 1997, the upper limit for partial selection by supposedly comprehensive schools would have been raised to 30% or to 50% if they were grant-maintained. Even then however, and certainly since, almost all specialist schools have insisted that they are and intend to remain truly comprehensive. If this had not been the case, there would surely have been more protests against Ministerial claims that while selecting on 'general academic ability' is invidious, doing so by aptitude for particular subjects as early as the age of 11 – by what Stephen Byers when he was Schools Minister defined as 'potential which might flourish and blossom if a child is exposed to particular types of education' – is feasible and fair. In the current DfEE list, eighteen of the twenty-two specialist comprehensives recorded as partly selecting their intakes were established before Labour took office, of which thirteen are former grant-maintained schools.

That most of them avoid even partial overt selection would seem to remove one otherwise obvious explanation of their relative success, although we believe that the conspicuous and vigorously publicised success of some specialist schools, particularly several city technology colleges, is inseparable from very untypical intakes. More generally, many more specialist schools have other less overt advantages in this respect. Curriculum specialisation has been defended as solving problems created by too much demand for successful schools in urban areas because they distribute choice across different kinds of school. Magnet Schools in the United States are often cited as an encouraging example, although claims that their specialised curriculum makes their intakes less socially segregated by attracting applications across traditional social class and ethnic lines have to be set against claims that they recruit more than their share of the ablest pupils and so increase the concentration of socially disadvantaged children in a 'residue' of non-specialist schools. Since 1997, when specialist schools generally had less than their 'share' of disadvantaged children, the Government has insisted on at least one such school in each Education Action Zone and has actively encouraged applications as part of its Excellence in Cities programme. It can therefore claim to be using specialist status partly to direct resources into disadvantaged areas. Although this may seem a rather clumsy mechanism for doing so, it will be interesting to compare the performance and improvement rates of these new arrivals with schools designated earlier. As a generalisation however, specialist schools are popular. Their popularity has some predictable effects on their intakes.

Those established schools included in Jesson's survey reported that their ratio of applications to places had risen towards two-to-one by 1998, and were inclined to attribute their improved market position partly to their specialism. Yet we have argued that there is little evidence that a specialised curriculum has significant influence on school choice, certainly not by comparison with such parental priorities as good results, a 'good' intake, and the likelihood that the child will be 'safe' and 'happy' there. Good facilities are also signi-ficant, particularly in areas (IT, science, sport and music) where specialisation is rewarded. Less tangibly, though no less powerfully, their officially recognised and locally publicised status may be seen by parents and children as indicating a 'better' school to be chosen because it is 'special' rather than 'specialised'. This is what hap-pened with city technology colleges. Undoubtedly popular with parents, they were attractive much less as a high-technology 'school of the future' (the Government's designation) than as the next level down from selective schools, despite being officially required to recruit intakes socially and academically 'representative' of their areas, and as a definite cut above 'ordinary' comprehensives nearby.[5] Somewhat similar perceptions benefited grant-maintained schools, even though parents were generally uninterested in or unimpressed by their greater autonomy. Since one source of distance from 'standard' comprehensives can build on another, it is perhaps not surprising that the proportion of grant-maintained and voluntary comprehensive schools among those designated by 1997 is much higher (just under 50%) than can be explained by the Conservatives' initial restriction of technology college status to those categories.

That the equivalent figure is less than a third among comprehensive schools designated since 1997 illustrates how the programme has broadened as well as increased its scope. Nevertheless, considerable room remains for less visible processes of selection and self-selec-tion to shape the social composition of school intakes. Popular schools may choose the more 'promising' applicants, using inter-views to identify those from the 'right kind' of home. Their popu-larity can lead less confident or less ambitious families to exclude themselves by not applying at all. In urban areas with strong com-petition for enough pupils to sustain viability and for children likely to enhance a school's future performance, the actual and potential advantages attached to specialist status seem to us to partly explain a distribution of specialist schools around the country. This is much more uneven than would be expected if individual schools had 'simply' made their decision to apply on educational grounds, with or without a keen eye on the extra resources which follow. As their comprehensive schools were identified in the GCSE performance tables last year, sixteen local authorities had none while another fifty-two had 81 between them. In contrast, thirty-one had more than six each and some 270 between them. We know that some Authorities discouraged applications, but doubt that this would have deterred schools determined to go ahead. It is more likely that successful applications have a snowball effect on other schools which fear being left behind. In the short run, removing the restriction on the proportion of pupils in specialist schools to not more than 30% of an LEA's total reduces the pressure to apply before leaving it too late. But it also highlights the prospect in the 2001 Green Paper of a tier of specialist schools as large as that containing the schools excluded or which exclude themselves. The implication already present in some publicising of the programme's success will then be very difficult to avoid – namely, that schools outside it lack the necessary quality, initiative and willingness to innovate. In short, their inferior resources and weaker reputation would be seen as deserved.

Our overriding concern is with that other half. It is why the programme's success cannot be fairly evaluated by citing its schools' better performance and faster improvement without taking account of its effects on 'standard' comprehensives at risk of being left behind. Ministers see it as a powerful mechanism for raising standards generally. We see it as potentially extremely divisive, and as one way of rationing on so far inadequate grounds the distribution of additional resources. Of course that view is open to being dismissed as an outdated objection to doing anything anywhere, or as inhibiting the best for the sake of the mediocre. Yet in the new Labour Government's first Education White Paper, the endemic problem with our education system was 'easily stated' as a preoccupation with 'excellence at the top' at the expense of the many.

John Major's vision of 'a grammar school in every town', for example, was conspicuously lacking in any complementary vision for the consequent secondary modern schools in those towns. Tony Blair dismissed it at the time, shortly before taking office, as reflecting the needs of 'a vanished society' in which a small educated elite managed a workforce equipped with no more than basic skills and a training in deferring to their betters.

Of course specialist schools are not grammar schools in disguise. But it would be ironic if Blair's Government raised a new tier of comprehensive schools above the rest, even one with a more even division between winners and losers than when selection flourished and where it still survives. The recent Green Paper refers, ambiguously, to a 'post-comprehensive era'. Specialist schools will be a critical ingredient in shaping that era. It is reasonable to expect the Government to explain why modernisation entails specialisation; if this is a self-evident proposition, then schools announcing a specialised curriculum would be expected in Scotland, in substantial numbers in Wales, and in the private sector. It is essential that it explains how the prospect of even more disproportionate numbers of the socially disadvantaged in 'second-best' schools will be avoided.

References

1. Anne West, Philip Noden, Mark Kleinman and Christine Whitehead, *Examining the Impact of the Specialist Schools Programme*. Centre for Educational Research, London School of Economics and Political Science, 2000 (DfEE Research Report RR196)

2. Tamsyn Imison and Tony Edwards, 'A new way to be divisive?' *Times Educational Supplement* 1 January 1999

3. Anthony Adonis and Stephen Pollard, *A Class Act: The Myth of Britain's Classless Society.* Penguin Books, 1998

4. David Jesson, 'That specialist smile' *Times Educational Supplement*, 16 February 2001; his statistical comparison of schools and LEAs with and without academic selection was reported in the same journal 3 March, 2000. A study of *Value-Added in Specialist Schools*, written with Sir Cyril Taylor, was published by the Technology Colleges Trust 1999

5. Geoff Whitty, Tony Edwards and Sharon Gewirtz, *Specialsation and Choice in Urban Education*. Routledge, 1993.

Notes on contributors

Geoff Carr is Deputy Head of a community school in Watford in Hertfordshire and a member of the Community Education Development Council (CEDC).

Clyde Chitty is currently Professor of Education and Head of the Department of Educational Studies at Goldsmiths College, University of London. He is the author, co-author or editor of over thirty books and reports on the history and politics of education, a member of the Socialist Teachers' Alliance and co-editor of the campaigning educational journal *Forum*.

Mike Davies has held headships in rural Scotland, inner London and Milton Keynes which have stimulated and given vent to two parallel passions: one, the development of school-based curriculum and pedagogy; and the other, the reculturing/restructuring of large secondary schools on a human scale. Board membership of the British Curriculum Foundation and Human Scale Movement reflect these long-term quests.

Jon Duveen is a biology teacher at the Sixth Form Centre of City and Islington College and an officer of the Islington Teachers Association (NUT).

Patrick Eavis was Headteacher of Manor Park Comprehensive School in Newcastle, and then, until 1997, of Queen Elizabeth High School, Hexham. Since then he has contributed regularly to the training of new teachers at Newcastle University, and has been actively involved in the national training programme for headteachers and aspiring headteachers.

Tony Edwards is Emeritus Professor of Education at Newcastle University. He has collaborated in evaluations of the Assisted Places Scheme and of City Technology Colleges, and more recently in a follow-up study of academically 'able' young people whose secondary education had been in private, grammar and comprehensive schools. Until 1998, he was Chair of Governors at Queen Elizabeth High School, Hexham.

Richard Hatcher a Senior Lecturer in Education at the University of Central England in Birmingham. He has written widely on education policy. He is founding co-editor of the journal *Education and Social Justice*.

Philippe Harari is a psychology teacher at Long Road Sixth Form College in Cambridge and Secretary of the Cambridge and District Association (NUT).

Ken Jones is a Senior Lecturer in Education at Keele University. He is co-editor of the journal *Education and Social Justice*. He taught in comprehensive schools in London for 15 years, and is the author of *Beyond Progressive Education* (1983) and *Right Turn: the Conservative Revolution in Education* (1989).

Rachel Jones is a secondary school teacher and an NUT officer in West London.

Carole Regan is a full-time teacher of GNVQ business and humanities at a girls' comprehensive school in Tower Hamlets. She was President of the National Union of Teachers, 1996/7. She is an elected member of the General Teaching Council and a member of the Socialist Teachers' Alliance.

Brian Simon is an eminent historian of British education and has been an active campaigner for comprehensive education since the early 1950s. His four-volume *Studies in the History of Education*, covering the years 1780 to 1990, is universally regarded as the standard work on the history of education in this country.

Margaret Tulloch has been on the Campaign for State Education National Executive for over 10 years. CASE campaigns for all children to be able to benefit from a fully-resourced comprehensive education, for a locally accountable education system and for a partnership between home, school and the community. Margaret is the governor of a comprehensive secondary and of primary schools in the London Borough of Merton.

Geoff Whitty is Director of the Institute of Education, University of London, having formerly been Karl Mannheim Professor of Sociology of Education. He is the author of a number of books and articles on the sociology and politics of education.

Bob Wood is Secretary of Leeds Central Constituency Labour Party and a supporter of Leeds CASE. He grew up in a single parent family in Southall, West London, and benefited from a grammar school education as much as his three siblings were disadvantaged by a secondary modern education.

John Yandell teaches at Kingsland School, Hackney; he is the editor of *Socialist Teacher.*